READER BONUS!

Dear Reader,

Learn the basics of resilience and engagement skills for college students so you can prepare yourself and your child for a fruitful academic year. Download a free copy of “College Survival Guide for Conservatives: 5 Easy and Practical Tips for Parents” along with a bonus coaching video at www.risestudentcoaching.com.

Discover the essential foundations of resilience and engagement skills specifically designed for college students, equipping both you and your child with the necessary tools for a successful and fulfilling academic year.

As an added bonus, gain invaluable insights through a coaching video accompanying the guide, ensuring you are well-equipped to navigate the unique challenges and opportunities that lie ahead. Don’t miss out on this opportunity to empower yourself and support your child’s journey through college.

If we are still giving away this course by the time you’re reading this book, head straight over to your computer and start the course now. It’s absolutely free and you’ll be glad you did.

READER BONUS!

Download the course here: www.risestudentcoaching.com

BOOKS COMING SOON!

TEACHER VOICES SILENCED

Delve into the behind-the-scenes experiences of conservative K-12 and university faculty as they share their firsthand accounts of keeping their traditional values and conservative views concealed while teaching in today's educational environment. Once discovered, the consequences are often extreme, including termination and "blacklisting."

PARENT VOICES SILENCED

Conservative parents, grandparents, aunts, uncles, and friends have been eliminated from the lives of their loved ones because of their conservative and traditional views and beliefs. Hear the heartbreaking stories of their loss and grief as they struggle to accept the destruction of the American Family as it plays out in their own lives. Family has been considered the core of society and the fabric that holds our country together. As it's being systematically dismantled, families live in despair, feeling helpless to attain peace or healing.

To address the deeply concerning issue of conservative individuals being excluded from the lives of their loved ones due to differing views and beliefs, it is crucial to foster dialogue, understanding, and empathy. The proposed solutions aim to rebuild fractured family relationships and promote harmony within communities. By focusing on communication, education, and community engagement, we can begin to restore the vital fabric of the American family, fostering healing, peace, and unity within our society.

Subscribe to updates and notifications at www.risestudentcoaching.com.

STUDENT VOICES SILENCED

The College Survival Guide
for Conservative Students
and Parents

STUDENT VOICES SILENCED

First-hand Accounts of Extreme Bias Every Conservative Parent Needs to Know and How to Navigate College Successfully

Publisher Email: lynda@actiontakerspublishing.com

Publisher Website: www.actiontakerspublishing.com

ISBN # (paperback) 979-8-9885219-0-7
ISBN # (Kindle) 979-8-9885219-1-4
Published by Action Takers Publishing™

Dedication

To my dad, Roger Ekstrand, thank you for teaching me the value of free and critical thinking. It was your religion. You were *always* dedicated to education and being a learned man. You would be disturbed to know that higher education has been hijacked to become a political weapon. You taught me to question and think for myself. Your example has led me on this journey.

To my mother, Darlene Ekstrand, thank you for showing kindness, love, and compassion. It's what drives my heart and passion to fight for these young people and their families who need advocates in an academic world that doesn't respect their morals, values, or their love of God. I take on this responsibility because you would want me to be brave and to follow my calling and my conscience.

To my husband, Tony, I thank you for showing me how to stand up and fight for what is right. Every day you model how to use a powerful voice to speak out for truth. You taught me how to bring the imagined "up out of the ground" - like a house - one 'stick' at a time. I never would have taken on this life-changing work without you. I thank you for saving me so many times. I love you for giving me roots and wings.

Acknowledgment

To the brave students, educators, and parents who have so graciously and courageously shared their stories with me, my heartfelt gratitude goes out to each of you. You go into battle every day that you step foot onto a university campus. Your experiences and stories are invaluable in the crusade to educate the uninformed, and prepare students and parents embarking on this journey. Without your words, this message would still be silenced.

To Lynda Sunshine West and Sally Green of Action Takers Publishing. You have been central in allowing this cause that's been swimming in my head to flourish into voice and words on paper. Thank you for your expertise, always so generously given, and for making this process heartfelt and fun.

Table of Contents

Dedication vii

Acknowledgment ix

Introduction 1

CHAPTER 1: My Voice at Last 5

CHAPTER 2: Parents Don’t Know How Bad It Is 15

CHAPTER 3: The System 33

CHAPTER 4: The Student 81

CHAPTER 5: Student Support 151

CHAPTER 6: Strategies 167

CHAPTER 7: Where to Begin: Challenge and Support 195

Introduction

"If the challenge is too great and the student is not ready for the challenge, a student may go into a state of retreat, where they cease to develop and pull away from the challenge." (Evans, 2010).

In the realm of higher education, colleges and universities have long been hailed as bastions of intellectual curiosity, critical thinking, and open dialogue. They are meant to be environments where diverse perspectives can co-exist, leading to a vibrant exchange of ideas and a fertile ground for personal growth. However, beneath this idealized façade, a troubling reality persists—one that has left many conservative students and their parents feeling voiceless, marginalized and often ostracized for their political leanings. The college experience, which should be a time of intellectual exploration and growth, has become a battleground for those who hold conservative values.

"Student Voices Silenced: The College Survival Guide for Conservative Students and Parents" is a compelling collection of firsthand accounts that shed light on the extreme bias experienced by conservative students on campuses across the country. This book offers a critical and sobering look at the experiences of conservative students who have been marginalized and dismissed. It also aims to serve as an invaluable survival guide, empowering conservative students and their parents with the knowledge and strategies they need to successfully navigate the challenging landscape of higher education.

Within these pages, you will find a collection of personal stories that illuminate the pervasive biases encountered by conservative students on campuses. These narratives, gathered from diverse individuals who have braved the ideological storm, reveal the various ways in which conservative voices are stifled, belittled, and even suppressed. From classrooms to student organizations, from social events to administrative policies, the range of experiences shared in this book will open your eyes to a troubling reality that demands attention. The narratives shared in this book provide a platform for these voices to be heard, ensuring that the experiences of conservative students and their parents are acknowledged, understood, and addressed. Instead of fostering intellectual curiosity and critical thinking, many colleges and universities have become echo chambers of progressive ideologies, stifling free speech and hindering academic diversity.

Throughout this guide, readers will discover stories that capture the frustrations, fears, and isolation that conservative students encounter on a daily basis. From biased professors and indoctrinating curricula to a hostile social environment and ideological echo chambers, the challenges faced by these students are multifaceted and profound. We delve into the emotional toll these experiences take and the toll it can have on their academic success, personal development, and mental well-being.

But this book is not simply a documentation of grievances. "Student Voices Silenced" is a call to action for conservative students and their parents, urging them to be aware of the challenges that lie ahead and to equip themselves with the tools necessary to navigate the often treacherous terrain of higher education. It is also designed to empower conservative students and their parents with practical strategies and actionable advice. Drawing upon the insights of those who have traversed these tumultuous paths, I present proven techniques for navigating the college landscape successfully, both academically and personally, for conservative students to thrive despite the challenges they may face.

"Student Voices Silenced" offers strategies for building resilience, finding allies, and maintaining one's intellectual integrity. It addresses the emotional toll that can accompany being silenced and marginalized and offers coping mechanisms to ensure that conservative students do not lose their voice or sense of self. While the focus is on conservative students, this guide also offers valuable insights for all parents who seek to support their children through the challenges they may face in higher education.

This book also serves as a wake-up call to parents who may be unaware of the challenges their conservative children face on campus. It provides insights into the ideological battles taking place in classrooms, dormitories, and student organizations, empowering parents to support and guide their children through these formative years.

"Student Voices Silenced" is not an attack on the principles of higher education or a call for ideological segregation. It is a passionate plea for intellectual diversity, the free exchange of ideas, and the inclusion of conservative voices in the pursuit of knowledge. It is a reminder that higher education should be a place where all perspectives are valued and respected, and where students are empowered to think critically and challenge prevailing narratives.

As we embark on this eye-opening journey through the experiences of conservative students, faculty, and parents, let us remember that a thriving democracy depends on a robust exchange of ideas. Let us strive to ensure that no voice is silenced, that no perspective is diminished, and that the college campus becomes a place where conservative students can confidently express their views, challenge prevailing narratives, and grow intellectually. I seek to amplify the voices that have been silenced for far too long, reclaiming the spirit of open dialogue and intellectual curiosity that should define our institutions of higher learning. Together, we can create a more inclusive, balanced, and vibrant educational landscape—one that values and respects the diverse range of perspectives that shape our society.

So, to all conservative students and parents, take heart. You are not alone, and your voices will not be silenced. Let this book be your guide on the path to success, empowerment, and the preservation of conservative values in the halls of higher education.

The brave individuals that agreed to share their stories did so under the condition of anonymity. The testimony, facts, and direct words of the contributors have sometimes been changed to protect the interviewee's privacy and identity. Some of their stories have been combined and consolidated into one, as their experiences were parallel and were woven together to safeguard them from retaliation by their institution, academic departments, faculty, and peers.

Several of the resources found during the research conducted throughout this project were found on the internet. To that end, some of the links may no longer be valid by the time you're reading this book. Therefore, I have included (where feasible) snapshots of the articles and resources mentioned.

Resources are identified with a footnote and can be found at www.RISEstudentcoaching.com/resources.

CHAPTER 1

My Voice at Last

"I don't know how to be silent when my heart is speaking."
Fyodor Destoevsky, White Nights

"To create something is to risk something.
To stand for something is to risk something."
Fr. Mike Schmitz

TRIGGER WARNING!

The contents of this book will offend and outrage some readers. If you consider yourself to be a far-left "woke" activist and educator, or a supporter of liberal indoctrination at the cost of instructing our college students to be free thinkers, free speakers, free citizens to live however they wish within the laws of this country, consider yourself warned. This book will trigger you.

Trigger warnings abound in higher education. Any lecture hall or classroom that you walk into that isn't filled with liberal propaganda are labeled with trigger warnings. Any topic that may be challenging to human sensitivities and emotions are considered a "trigger" and students, faculty, or staff are offered the opportunity to not enter the room or to dismiss themselves to avoid potential emotional upset. The warnings, however, never apply to traditional or conservative students or university professionals. Those conservative participants must sit and endure all language, images, and messaging that is dictated by the liberals running the room. Conservatives are not allowed to leave the room. If they do, they run the risk of retaliation in the form of lowered academic grades, lost professional promotions, awards, and recognition. No "trigger" warnings for them.

You think it's just "over there" or at "that school"? It's not. With few exceptions, every campus waves their "Woke University" flag above any other flag. In fact, at one major public university located in the Western United States, a university staff member, who happens to be a marine veteran, was assisting with parents and students during the residence hall move-in process by transporting their boxes and gear across campus. He was stopped by an upper university administrator, and was told to remove the American flags he'd attached with zip ties from the golf cart he was using, because the American flag would be offensive to the parents and students. Rainbow pride flags, though, were displayed throughout campus and waved in the welcome parade.

Campuses have reinforced a culture of distinct groups and sub-groups. The groups deemed "underrepresented" have an advocacy platform that's respected and promoted. One of the few groups that is an exception is conservative or traditional groups. Although publicly recognized in marketing and advertising materials, in practice, overt and covert biases and microaggressions exist.

As with all groups, conservative and traditional groups are composed of many individuals who may or may not identify with all of the principles associated with the "group." Prevailing biases against conservatives on campus are so extreme, little leeway is allowed for individual differences or unique beliefs and values.

This causes a chasm between conservatives and liberals and prevents honest discourse between students and their peer group as well as with their instructors. This climate fosters exclusion and compromises the success that is deserving of all students attending college. *Students and parents need to be armed with facts and information to guide their actions, choices, and communications.*

The liberal movement was initiated on college campuses from earlier centuries. This was a natural outgrowth of edgy new thought driven by cutting edge ideas throughout history. Evaluating presumed facts through the lens of new theories and research is the foundation of progress. This progress has benefited our world in innumerable ways.

When I was a year and a half old, my mother survived cancer in an era when a cancer diagnosis meant certain death. Few were lucky enough to live through the extremely invasive surgery and radiation treatments. She's now in her 90s! I am forever grateful that I was blessed to be raised by this amazing woman. Institutional research, innovative ideas and advanced thought have proved necessary for countless advancements in medicine, technology, engineering, human longevity and quality of life.

I don't seek to throw the baby out with the bathwater. I do, however, encourage a socially imposed limit placed upon the liberal programming of our students. Serving 20 years in higher education as a mid-level administrator in Student Affairs, I observed a cultural shift that failed to support conservative and traditional students on campus and it infuriated me; hence, I decided to write this book. These students have become an "out group" and this culture on campus has caused students to consider self-harm, to drop-out, and to experience severe isolation.

I understand because this *is* my story. This is my story, the story of thousands of other faculty, staff, and administrators who are committed to higher education, committed to their students, and who sit silently in rooms, sitting on their hands, biting their tongues with their heart shrinking and their minds twirling, wondering how did things ever get like this? Admittedly, I did work on an extremely liberal campus for 15 years. However, having attended numerous national conferences and collaborating with colleagues across the country, I know absolutely that the liberal woke indoctrination happens on every campus, with very few exceptions. We conservatives have seen it happen and we have been left with few resources to assist our students.

It was anguish to go to work every day. Not because of the students. It was torture because of the environment and the administrators in power. An example that best illustrates the university environment was a workshop that was held for mid and upper administrators in student affairs. The workshop was held in April 2017 and was a "launch" planning session for the 2018 fall semester. A common practice in Student Affairs is an opening exercise "to bring everyone's voice into the room." Standing in small groups next to butcher paper taped to the walls around the room, we were all asked to record the successes and challenges we'd experienced throughout the year and brainstorm solutions for the upcoming year. When finished, we were all seated and each group presented in turn. After several groups had shared their professional struggles and victories, a Vice Chancellor's group was next. She took the lead, stood up, and started ranting about how upset she was, and that she had just spent the weekend grieving over the President of the United States. He made her so angry that he had destroyed her semester. She shouted, "I am ashamed to be an American." In tears and out of control, she waved her arms in the air, continuing on and growling, "It's unbelievable that so many idiotic, ignorant people could possibly have voted for *that* man, that Cheto!"

I sat staring down at my knees holding my coffee cup. Tears welling in *my* eyes now. Never at work had I ever felt so demoralized or so judged unfairly. Never had I felt so trapped and put into a box stamped "IDIOT! STUPID! IGNORANT!" I could be reprimanded or corrected by a supervisor over work performance; I could have disagreements with co-workers, but never had I felt so disrespected, so judged and so terrified. At that moment, I knew that my job relied not on my devotion to students, creating great work, or dedication to higher education. My job relied on me keeping my mouth shut and my head down.

Before that day, I had never considered myself a conservative. I've been a moderate my entire life. I believed that my civic duty was *not* to identify with a party or "a side," but to vote consistently in every election based upon my values, on the economic status at the time, the needs of my school district, my county, my city, my state, my country. I have voted Republican. I have voted Democrat. I have voted countless times for candidates of several parties believing that that was the right thing to do. I never believed in party politics. I believed that party politics got in the way of getting things done. That day, that moment, I knew we were in a war and I had to pick a side. I chose with my heart, mind, values, and conscience. That day I became a conservative and allied with a party, started researching conservative issues, and began watching a new TV channel for news.

Countless nights I went home and cried. I became depressed and withdrawn. At work it was hard for me to concentrate. I had anxiety any time I had to walk into a room for a meeting (of which there are endless meetings in higher education).

While writing this book, I conducted countless hours of research and discovered that I am not alone. I've spoken to numerous higher education professionals who feel the same way. We duck under the radar when we know that our tenure is on the line, our promotions, faculty recognition or awards all are compromised because of our political views. Survival tells us to be quiet and sit down.

Everyone deserves to be evaluated on their work and on their own merits as a person. We all need to be respected for who we are, how we identify as individuals. They strip away your identity and replace it with an identity that they approve of. During the "wokewave," my "husband" and I were married and I was thrilled. Of course my heart wanted to celebrate! It was a beautiful event that had happened in our lives. But, on campus, we were not allowed to call one another husband' and 'wife.' At work we were required to use the term 'partner,' because it might make homosexuals feel bad. We'd been whitewashed and neutered. It goes without saying that if one can't say "husband or wife," then surely we must announce our pronoun before every meeting or discussion, just in case one of us, or someone else in the room, had switched our sexual identity since the meeting the previous week.

When I felt so much pain, frustration, and disrespect as a mature adult professional who had coping skills, how in the world could these students navigate these complex dynamics of cultural power on campus? I did see students suffer. I saw students drop out. I saw them emotionally and psychologically withdraw. I saw them shrink as people as they had to pull themselves inward just to cope and survive, to not be noticed or called out.

I worked with a student who had a strong Christian faith. He went home every weekend to go to church with his family and have dinner at his grandma's. He told me that he felt so embarrassed about his strong Christian faith and values in this environment. He found that there was no place for him on campus. He had no adult advocates, no professionals that would help him because he was too white, too mainstream, too normal, too traditional, too conservative. He would come into my office to talk to me and I supported him as best I could, but I couldn't fix the problem. The problem was the institution. The problem was the culture, and he felt so isolated and alone that he was unable to interpret it all on his own. He needed guideposts to successfully navigate this new world. While his parents are great advocates, he needed someone other than them that he could trust. I was there with him every step of the way. He was a student who had worked hard through high school to save money to go to college and even worked a gap year at a fast food restaurant after high school just so he would be able to afford to live in the dorms with the other freshmen. It was such a disappointment to him because he was an outcast. He was in the "out group," and he eventually dropped out.

A couple of years later, one morning over breakfast, I was lamenting to my husband that these students were still left on campus; they were still trapped there! Because I retired and was able to leave, I had gotten away, but they were still there, every day struggling with the same challenges and biases that I had. Things hadn't gotten better - they'd gotten worse! He looked at me and said, "You have your own coaching and training business now, so why don't you do something about it? Why don't you help them? Why don't you provide coaching and training for parents and students?"

That simple suggestion while sipping our morning coffee has morphed into RISE (Resilience and Independence Skills for Engagement). RISE is both my coaching program for parents and students, as well as my coaching training program (RISE Coach Training) where I train coaches on the unique RISE program. RISE, an exclusive resilience-based coaching program for students and parents, is a navigation system to guide them through the maze of campus experiences and lead them on pathways to success.

Alone, I can only help a limited number of families. My coaching training program, RISE Coach Training, however, shares my expertise, materials, and resources with other coaches so students and parents can find the support and assistance they need to successfully navigate the challenges of campus and of this woke culture.

This book will offer you insights into life on campus and in today's classrooms. Rather than focusing on the facts and figures that are easily found online, this book is a narrative that sheds light on the truth of conservative experiences on campuses today told through personal accounts and firsthand experiences. I have interviewed dozens of faculty, parents, and students. All have asked that their identity be protected for fear of retaliation by their respective campuses. Names have been changed and some stories have been merged into composites. Most of the themes ran parallel to one another and only the details varied. Those stories have been merged for the reader's ease and for brevity. They will, nonetheless, enlighten parents, students, faculty, campus personnel, teachers, and personal coaches.

The aim of this book is to equip you with the necessary resources and advice to provide your student with the highest quality education possible.

In this book you will:

- **hear firsthand experiences of conservative students, parents, and faculty** so that you and your student are prepared;
- **master the language and culture** of today's college campuses to ensure success in the classroom;

- **learn the undesirable faculty and staff biases** that will be applied to your conservative student, so he or she knows what's to come and won't be blindsided, but, rather, will be prepared;
- **prime your student for success in making and keeping friendships** both online and in person;
- **gain insight into current student and faculty demographics**;
- **understand the basic student development theories** that serve as the underpinnings of higher education; and
- **recognize the importance of coaching** in your student's success trajectory and receive a valuable coaching video download to get you started (see the Reader Bonus at the very beginning of this book).

How to use this book:

I compulsively write in my books. Every margin is crammed with jottings, ideas, arrows, question marks, exclamation points, and a "to do" bullet list. This is especially true in books that prompt me to action and engage my passions. I hope this book becomes that for you. I hope it finds a home on a coffee table or night stand to be a reference guide for your child's college years.

Each page is designed with a wide margin to welcome those notes and ideas. Perhaps this book will serve as a diary, a guidebook, or a resource for conversations you'll have with campus personnel. You may find ideas that you want to note and share with other parents. This book is your friend and will allow you restful nights.

The following page shows you how to use the book taking advantage of the wide margin for note taking. Grab your highlighters and colored pens. Enjoy the process and enjoy the book!

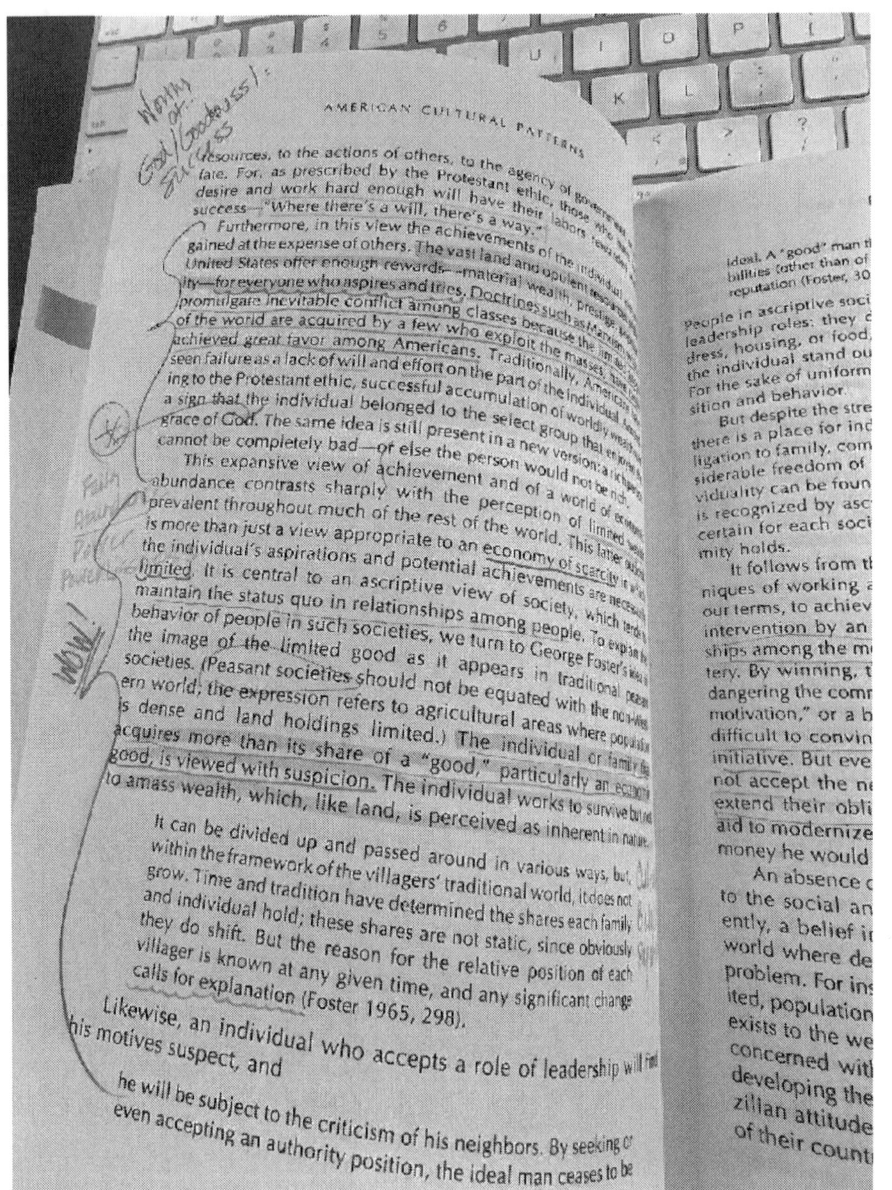

AMERICAN CULTURAL PATTERNS

resources, to the actions of others, to the agency of government or fate. For, as prescribed by the Protestant ethic, those who desire and work hard enough will have their labors rewarded with success—"Where there's a will, there's a way."

Furthermore, in this view the achievements of the individual are not gained at the expense of others. The vast land and opulent resources of the United States offer enough rewards—material wealth, prestige, popularity—for everyone who aspires and tries. Doctrines such as Marxism that promulgate inevitable conflict among classes because the limited goods of the world are acquired by a few who exploit the masses, have not achieved great favor among Americans. Traditionally, Americans have seen failure as a lack of will and effort on the part of the individual. According to the Protestant ethic, successful accumulation of worldly wealth was a sign that the individual belonged to the select group that enjoyed the grace of God. The same idea is still present in a new version: a rich person cannot be completely bad—or else the person would not be rich.

This expansive view of achievement and of a world of economic abundance contrasts sharply with the perception of limited wealth prevalent throughout much of the rest of the world. This latter outlook is more than just a view appropriate to an economy of scarcity in which the individual's aspirations and potential achievements are necessarily limited. It is central to an ascriptive view of society, which tends to maintain the status quo in relationships among people. To explain the behavior of people in such societies, we turn to George Foster's idea of the image of the limited good as it appears in traditional peasant societies. (Peasant societies should not be equated with the non-Western world; the expression refers to agricultural areas where population is dense and land holdings limited.) The individual or family that acquires more than its share of a "good," particularly an economic good, is viewed with suspicion. The individual works to survive but not to amass wealth, which, like land, is perceived as inherent in nature.

> It can be divided up and passed around in various ways, but, within the framework of the villagers' traditional world, it does not grow. Time and tradition have determined the shares each family and individual hold; these shares are not static, since obviously they do shift. But the reason for the relative position of each villager is known at any given time, and any significant change calls for explanation (Foster 1965, 298).

Likewise, an individual who accepts a role of leadership will find his motives suspect, and

> he will be subject to the criticism of his neighbors. By seeking or even accepting an authority position, the ideal man ceases to be

ideal. A "good" man t
bilities (rather than of
reputation (Foster, 30

People in ascriptive soci
leadership roles: they c
dress, housing, or food,
the individual stand ou
For the sake of uniform
sition and behavior.

But despite the stre
there is a place for ind
ligation to family, com
siderable freedom of
viduality can be foun
is recognized by asc
certain for each soci
mity holds.

It follows from t
niques of working
our terms, to achiev
intervention by an
ships among the m
tery. By winning,
dangering the comr
motivation," or a b
difficult to convin
initiative. But eve
not accept the n
extend their obli
aid to modernize
money he would

An absence
to the social an
ently, a belief i
world where de
problem. For ins
ited, population
exists to the we
concerned wit
developing the
zilian attitude
of their count

CHAPTER 2

Parents Don't Know How Bad It Is

In a conversation with a professor with nearly two decades of experience, he described his campus experience:

"In 2016 I would have identified as middle of the road, politically. I've always been independent. I voted on issues and policies rather than specific political parties or platforms. I have my own personal values and beliefs. I vote according to my personal wisdom and experience as well as doing my own research and remaining informed about issues.

"Then Trump was elected. The entire campus reacted in horror. Half the faculty called out sick. In conversations with other faculty, they described Trump voters as "despicable." I have family members that are republican and they're not despicable, ignorant, intolerant, racist, or any of the other judgments that were being made. Those faculty are intolerant, mean, and judgmental. They failed to see their own biases. That's the day I changed.

"They said such horrible things about middle American voters. Many of the students we serve are from middle America. The parents that pay the mighty tuition dollars are from middle America. Students started privately complaining to me that entire classes were exclusively about Trump. No other learning was taking place. Students were forced to sit there day after day listening to professors indoctrinate them against their families, their morals, the core of themselves.

"And then George Floyd happened and everything intensified. Absolutely, whenever a life is lost needlessly it is a tragedy, but the consequential violence and lawlessness that unfolded was horrendous. The divide grew into a chasm that no one could bridge. Campus blew up and was ruled by divisiveness and elitism. The only topics that were acceptable to discuss were racism and climate change, and it became acceptable to do whatever it took to push these issues to the forefront of everything, at the sacrifice of real education.

"Academia then wholeheartedly embraced Critical Race Theory. This theory goes against everything that's true morally and ethically in our society. Historically, yes, atrocities were perpetrated. Are there pockets of racism that exist today? Of course. The systemic racism theory that was being dispensed in the classroom was entirely wrong. It's a THEORY, but wasn't taught as such. Faculty are arrogant to start with. But with the Black Lives Matter movement behind them, they were untouchable and could justifiably teach anything they chose."

Every conservative parent needs to know what their child will be encountering when they step onto campus. It's challenging for adults to maintain their moral compass when they are bombarded with opposing viewpoints. Few fully developed adults, when confronted by an adverse group, will be able to maintain their opinions without sliding into a gray area or becoming indecisive. Students in this very critical stage of their development are more susceptible to a blurring of values. It is necessary for every parent to understand what happens behind the scenes on college campuses and do everything possible to prepare and support their student through the "woke maze" and intentional indoctrination.

It's inexcusable that any college student should feel unsafe and threatened on campus. It's unconscionable that these behaviors and attitudes are supported and even motivated by administration and faculty. Students go to college seeking knowledge, wisdom, and experience. The current campus culture offers them a biased, prejudiced, and divisive community created by the professionals in positions of power.

Students who feel physically threatened, emotionally compromised, and isolated will likely not thrive in this environment. How can they be expected to achieve and succeed academically, socially, and developmentally when they are being told they are wrong, evil, and bad? How can they invest in a legacy of success and social contribution when they are set apart and cast into an uncompromising category of unworthiness and dishonor?

As a staff member of a top tier university, every individual (student, staff, faculty, or administration) had a required number of diversity and inclusion training hours to fulfill each year. It was a "whether you need it or not" attitude. Whether or not you had attended the same workshop the previous two years, you were still required to go each time it was offered. HR departments had been expanded in order to accommodate training on new "woke" subjects. Records were kept with lists of attendees with notations made of participation levels and any dissenting comments and they went into an employee record. This is the slow indoctrination that happens on campus. It begins innocuously. Of course everyone wants to improve their job performance and should grow as professionals. The sense of helplessness is overwhelming for students, faculty and staff that aren't of the same belief system to endure countless hours of this training.

[1] *If you're affiliated with a college or university and it initiates a set of diversity training, you probably won't bring up research suggesting that these trainings either have a negligible impact on racial attitudes or make them worse. People might conclude that you don't support diversity, period. That's just too big a risk to take, especially if you don't have seniority or tenure.*

Even with seniority or tenure, departments and administrative offices are restructured to justify the elimination of individuals that don't adhere to the agenda.

Equity was more important than fair-mindedness. Diversity was more important than mutual respect. Social change was more important than honoring one's cultural traditions and values. Survey stats were more important than an individual's unique experience. The one university's official website states as a top priority, "Move accountability for diversity and inclusion from the periphery to core institutional function." Their "Campus Blueprint for Diversity, Inclusion, and *Academic Excellence"* does not identify a single goal to achieve academic success.

One professor shared her views on Higher Education, "Higher Ed is the biggest joke now. People on the outside just don't know. They send their kids to have the same college experience they had. It just doesn't exist anymore; not in any way. Their students will come back as a different person. They force students to believe that they're horrible people. They will be against their traditional values. They have to be to survive. They have to be to get a passing grade. The pervasive campus culture is upending their moral compass. Sending their kids to college now is a deal with the devil. Everything I believed about education

1 www.RISEstudentcoaching.com/resources

doesn't exist - higher education is dead! I'm disgusted by what my own profession has become.

"The campus experience is unrecognizable to the older generations. Higher Ed is toxic. Parents are financially supporting their students to become a different person."

You'll find your biggest clues in plain sight when you visit campus. Many campuses fly rainbow pride flags, and Black Lives Matter banners are in full view hanging in dorm room windows. Stating your preferred pronouns will be a requirement on your visit. Your tour may include visiting gender-neutral bathrooms, the LGBTQ+ office, the office of diversity, equity and inclusion, and you may even stop by the foot-washing basin next to the Muslim prayer room.

[2]As described by NPR, "A Muslim ritual called 'wudu' is a tradition that involves washing one's hands, face and feet before prayers. In an effort to be sensitive to this practice, a number of colleges and universities have constructed foot baths to accommodate Muslim students. Some argue that the foot baths aren't needed and that they violate separations of religion and state, as state funds or student fees pay for these renovations."

On your campus tour, however, you'll be challenged to find any symbols of Christianity or Christian designated spaces. Holiday observances have been stripped of any Christian traditions or symbols. Campus dining halls celebrate Hindu holidays, Muslim holidays, African holidays, Irish holidays, Himalayan holidays, Native American holidays, but not conventional Christian holidays.

All incoming students are required to attend a campus orientation to "understand the campus culture." Sometimes offered online and

---

2 www.risestudentcoaching.com/resources

sometimes on campus, students will be introduced to the campus culture, rules, resources, and advising. Culture and rules are both overt and covert at these gatherings and training. Some of them happen through the welcome process. Others are through their housing staff. Mandatory meetings for all students living in the Halls are held by RAs and Hall directors. These meetings directly define the rules of campus and the rules of housing. This sets the stage for the expectations of student behavior and communication on these floors.

Defining the community is helpful, unless your culture, your values and morals fall outside of the boundaries of those established by the university and housing staff. Students are expected to sit and listen to the expectations such as defining your pronouns, understanding white privilege, respecting the needs of marginalized students before the needs of white students.

These orientations also emphasize the campus code of conduct. Students are expected to know the defined rules that the campus has established and the consequences of behaving outside of those rules. Having looked at many campus codes of conduct, I noticed some similarities. These similarities include honesty, trust, respect, fairness, responsibility, integrity, justice, equality, compassion in human relations, respecting dignity of all persons, accepting individual differences, respecting the environment and the rights of others, excellence, accountability, and service.

The Code of Conduct on one campus on the East Coast states, "When faced with adversity students will engage in thoughtful reflection and exhibit superior ethical decision-making skills. They respect the rights and dignity of all members of our community by listening attentively, communicating clearly and remaining open to understanding others."

Riley Gaines, a championship women's swimmer who has been speaking out against trans women's rights to compete against biological women in collegiate sports, put San Francisco State's Student Code of Conduct to the test. On a speaking tour with Turning Point USA, in April 2023, Gaines was confronted by an angry mob of protesters and assaulted by a man wearing a dress. Identifying as a trans woman and in protest to Gaines' Speech for women's rights, he beat her physically, and traumatized her mentally. The official university response was sent via email to the student body claiming that the student protests were peaceful despite video footage that filmed the attack.

David Llamas, TPUSA Field Representative posted this email to Twitter. The university's email states, "*But we may also find ourselves exposed to divergent views and even views we find personally abhorrent*," according to Llamas. "*These encounters have sometimes led to discord, anger, confrontation and fear. We must meet this moment and unite with a shared value of learning. Thank you to our students who participated peacefully in Thursday evening's event. It took tremendous bravery to stand in a challenging space. I am proud of the moments where we listened and asked insightful questions. I am also proud of the moments when our students demonstrated the value of free speech and the right to protest peacefully. These issues do not go away, and these values are very much at our core.*" No other action has been taken by the University.[3]

San Francisco State University's Code of Conduct reads,

"The University is committed to maintaining a safe and healthy living and learning environment for students, faculty, and staff. Each member of the campus community should choose behaviors that contribute toward this end. Students are expected to be good citizens

3 www.RISEstudentcoaching.com/resources

and to engage in responsible behaviors that reflect well upon their university, to be civil to one another and to others in the campus community, and contribute positively to student and university life."

One must assume that the students involved in this protest had not read the student code of conduct, or the institution had not enforced its rules and expectations consistently enough that these students believed that they were not required to comply with their own campus code of conduct.

Ask yourself, or better yet the host on your campus tour, if your conservative student will receive impartial treatment from liberal professors such as this one at Kent State. A recent article reports the hatred bordering on criminal incitement expressed by a faculty member.

[4]WJBK March 27, 2023 (Fox News, Detroit) said the professor, Steven Shaviro, posted a message on his personal Facebook page that addressed "right-wing" speakers being allowed on University campuses.

The station said the message began with, "So here is what I think about free speech on campus. Although I do not advocate violating federal and state criminal codes, I think it is far more admirable to kill a racist, homophobic, or transphobic speaker than it is to shout them down. When right-wing groups invite such speakers to campus, it is precisely because they want to provoke an incident that discredits the left, and gives more publicity and validation to these reprehensible views than they could otherwise attain," the station's screenshot shows.

4 www.RISEstudentcoaching.com/resources

Steven Shaviro

1d ·

So here is what I think about free speech on campus. Although I do not advocate violating federal and state criminal codes, I think it is far more admirable to kill a racist, homophobic, or transphobic speaker than it is to shout them down.

"The protesters get blamed instead of the bigoted speaker; the university administration finds a perfect excuse to side publicly with the racists or phobes; the national and international press has a field day saying that the bigots are the ones being oppressed, rather than the people those bigots actually hate being the victims of oppression," WJBK's screenshot adds.

The post, according to the station's screenshot, also reads, "In short, every time protesters shout down a racist or transphobic speaker, they are indulging their own moral sense of validity at the expense of actually strengthening the very bigots against whom they are protesting."

Steven Shaviro

1d ·

So here is what I think about free speech on campus. Although I do not advocate violating federal and state criminal codes, I think it is far more admirable to kill a racist, homophobic, or transphobic speaker than it is to shout them down.

When right-wing groups invite such speakers to campus, it is precisely because they want to provoke an incident that discredits the left, and gives more publicity and validation to these reprehensible views than they could otherwise attain. The protesters get blamed instead of the bigoted speaker; the university administration finds a perfect excuse to side publicly with the racists or phobes; the national and international press has a field day saying that bigots are the ones being oppressed, rather than the people those bigots actually hate being the victims of oppression.

In short, every time protestors shout down a racist or transphobic speaker, they are indulging their own moral sense of validity at the expense of actually strengthening the very bigots against whom they are protesting.

The exemplary historical figure in this regard is Sholem Schwarzbard, who assassinated the anti-Semitic butcher Symon Petliura, rather than trying to shout him down. Remember that Schwarzbard was acquitted by a jury, which found his action justified.

 57 92 comments 35 shares

  Share

Steven Shaviro

1d ·

As an alternative to Perry White's exclamation "Great Caesar's Ghost!", I have always liked "Suffering Sunbeam!" (which as far as I know was only used as an

Imagine if your child was the student bringing conservative speakers to this campus and had this professor as an instructor. He was eventually suspended, but the damage had already been done.

Tabling

The tradition of "tabling" on university campuses has been used for several decades as a means of engaging with students, promoting causes, and raising awareness about various issues. While it is difficult to pinpoint an exact starting point for this tradition, tabling has been a common practice on campuses for a significant amount of time.

Tabling typically involves setting up a table, usually in common areas such as student centers or cafeterias. This allows for students to obtain information about various organizations and activities, recruit members, and network with other groups. Tables may include informational pamphlets, flyers, and posters. In addition to providing basic information about an organization or activity, tabling can be used to collect signatures for petitions, discuss opportunities available with the organization or activity, provide a space to learn more about upcoming events or activities related to the organization, and serve as a source of advice and support to members of the community. Tabling is often used by student organizations as part of their recruitment efforts. By providing a physical presence on campus they increase their visibility and become better known in the campus community. Additionally, tabling can be used to raise awareness about important issues in the campus community and generate discussion among peers about those topics.

One recent graduate, Ryan, told of his experience during the elections of 2016 at a midwestern university while 'tabling.' He and other student members of College Republicans were 'tabling' at their campus student union. A professor approached them, leaned over their table and sneered at the students, "Why are you F…ing morons? You're so F….ing stupid!" He and the other students were also shouted at by other students passing by, being called the stereotypical conservative epithets including, "RACIST! HOMOPHOBE! NAZI!"

When a student attacks another student, either verbally or to inflict physical harm, the attacker could potentially be entered into the campus restorative justice system. Restorative justice seeks to examine the harmful impact of a crime or incident and then determines what can be done to repair that harm while holding the person who caused it accountable for his or her actions. Accountability for the offender means accepting responsibility and acting to repair the harm done.

What this means in simple terms is that University personnel sit down with the victim to understand how they felt, how they were affected, and what the ongoing impacts are in several areas of their life from the event. Then the restorative justice official meets with the offending person or group, and through talking sessions, the official tries to get them to understand the impact the offender had on the victims.

Then they meet together and, in essence, the offending group apologizes for what they did. If there's any possible way that they could make amends or reparations those arrangements are made.

In the example of the students who were shouted at *all day* long by their peers passing by and shouting at them, it would be impossible under this restorative justice system to stop each student shouting "Nazi" or "Homophobe" and send them through the restorative justice system. That is unrealistic and would be an administrative nightmare. It would be impossible for the students that are tabling to report every student passing by. In this type of situation, it would be inconceivable to hold each offender accountable for their actions and encourage them to take responsibility for their behavior and to make amends to those affected by it.

In addition to its primary focus of restoring relationships, restorative justice also provides an opportunity for community healing, understanding, and growth. For that goal to be met, social norms and campus policies need to be constructed and upheld at the highest levels of the university. There can be no question in students' minds that this type of behavior is disrespectful and unacceptable. For students to gain respect for the student code of conduct, it would be enforced heavily by the university. But, instead, it is enforced like Swiss cheese. There are some students held to high account. Others to no account. Campus bias is evidenced regularly by conservative students.

These incidents are happening every day on University campuses. If your student is not the student who is publicly taking action and speaking out, then your student is the one in their room or their apartment keeping silent and suffering alone. From your child's standpoint, they see only three options: (1) keep silent and suffer alone, (2) stand up for their beliefs and risk mental, emotional, and/or physical harm, or (3) conform to the liberal ways and change their belief system, the one you instilled in them since birth.

As you can imagine, anxiety is high for students. In general, mental health is a serious issue on campuses today. As our common language continues to evolve and become more "woke," students' confidence decreases and anxiety increases as they fear innocently having a conversation with a professional staff, faculty or other students. The most fundamental things such as having an uncomplicated conversation can be threatening.

Common instructions you'll hear around campus regarding language usage is:

- "Free speech is bad!"
- "Speech is violence!"
- "Never assume someone's gender or use the incorrect gender pronoun!"
- "Don't say 'folks,' say 'folx;' it's more inclusive!"
- "Don't single out 'People, guys, or girls,' call them 'Humans'!"
- "Never call someone a 'Jew,' they are 'Jewish people'!"
- "If you must use 'Woman,' correct it to 'Womxn' to cross out the '*man*'!"
- "Don't say, 'Latino' or 'Latina,' use 'Latinx' instead. It's more inclusive!"
- "Instead of 'Mother,' call that person your 'Birthing parent'!"
- "Instead of 'Father,' call that person your 'Non-gestational parent'!"
- "Don't assume anyone's sexuality. They may be 'pansexual' and not have a sexual preference!"
- "Never say 'breastfeeding,' instead use 'chestfeeding' because not all feeders have breasts."
- "Language hurts people's feelings if you have more privilege than they do!"
- "Don't wear that costume! It's cultural appropriation!"
- "Indigenous People lived on this campus' land! Repeat the campus' 'Land Acknowledgement' before every meeting begins!"

- "A lot of students struggle with intersectionality. They aren't just one simple identity!"
- "If you use that language, I feel marginalized!"
- "If you can't even see the systemic oppression, it's because you're part of it!"
- "Don't say heterosexual, use 'cysgender' instead."
- "Don't say, 'him' or 'her,' that excludes gender binary students!"
- "Just because I sleep with a lot of guys, don't 'slut shame' me!"
- "Stay away from men who have 'toxic masculinity.' They're bad!"
- "I'd hate to be a 'white feminist'! They're such fakes!"

Students have to be self-censoring constantly, and without complete understanding of the rules, norms, and expectations. They're left feeling anxious, afraid and eventually they shut down. When they observe other students being attacked and vilified while in a group, their natural reaction typically is to isolate, be alone, or to switch and become the other side; try and blend in, and try to be 'normal.' There begins the progression of denying their own morals, values, and beliefs. They leave the familiar and conventional and begin to embrace the unconventional. They have no choice. It's a survival skill. It's a coping skill that shouldn't be necessary on our campuses today.

For young women it's confusing. They're being given mixed messages. Am I a woman? Am I not a woman? Am I a feminist? Am I not a feminist? What are those definitions? Am I an old fashioned feminist like my Mom's era, or am I a new feminist? How do I identify? Identifying as anything other than mainstream, normative, hetero is now considered the coolest thing!

Still needing peer group approval, young women believe that it is a natural part of their process to question their sexual identity. Young women who just assume they are "Cys" or "Cysgender" women now are considered foolish or frightened for not going through a process of examining their sexual identity through a woke lens. Men are an enemy and something to be frightened of unless they pledge that they, too, are feminists and are questioning their sexuality.

Anyone who has experienced sexual violence or inappropriate and unwanted advances understands the impact that has on one's confidence, self-esteem, and on your perceived ability to protect your own body. Thankfully, campuses have stood up and began enforcing very strict policies on sexual harassment and violence.

From one young man's point of view, however, it has taken another turn. Ryan shared his experience going to the campus gym. He was observing young women with their phones posting videos of the young men there in the event that any of the men looked over at the young women. If they looked over, it was interpreted as ogling, which is now categorized as inappropriate and potentially violent.

He said, "They are being ridiculous. We're all humans in the same space. Nowadays, guys are okay with being single; it's safer than being with women. So many girls say, 'you suck, men suck, we don't want to be around you.' I think that all of this compromises them because when they're in a real dangerous situation, no one's going to believe them. They say anytime a guy looks their way he's attacking them. It's like crying wolf."

Parents don't know how bad it is and that their children are in a bind. There are a lot of things that children are willing to tell their parents, but too much about the challenges of their college experience puts them in another threatening situation. If their parents are footing the bill and paying for them to be there, telling their parents how unhappy they are and how challenging the campus is, is interpreted *to them* as telling their parents that they want to leave or that they should leave. And worst of all, that they can't handle it and are failing 'at college.'

Are students being put in a situation that they are not yet able to navigate alone? If they tell their parents how bad it is, is there anything their parents can really do? If their parents come to campus and complain, they make things even worse for their child. If they pull the funding and take them home, the student loses their hopes and dreams and ultimately leaves them feeling like they have failed. If they complain or try to take action on their own on campus, there are no advocates for conservative students; there's no one to help them.

They want to succeed, they want to graduate, they want to make friends, they want to have a social life, they want to make memories, they want to have that great college experience that everyone talks about. So the alternative that so often appears to be the best choice to a student is either to retreat and just keep their head down and endure it silently, or to embrace the new liberal progressive values and fit in.

Parents and students don't have to navigate this alone. It's important to know that university personnel, without question and with very few exceptions, are not *your* friend, and they're not *your* advocate. For conservative parents and students, the university is not going to go to bat for you. They're going to tell your student that they need to learn a different way of being, they need to learn to comply, they need to learn how to compromise, and they need to learn how to conform. For parents and students to navigate this reality:

1) prepare the student as best you can before they leave for college;

2) be ready with support strategies; and

3) work with a coach that specializes in working with conservative parents and students in colleges and universities, such as the RISE Student Coaching program.

Too many students and parents are struggling alone. They don't have to. RISE Student Coaching is here to help.

CHAPTER 3

The System

Students Are Emotionally Harmed and Physically Threatened

INSTITUTIONAL BIAS

[5]55.1% of campus conservatives say they're too scared to speak or show their political identity to even their friends, contrasted with 60% of Democratic students that say they feel they can share their opinions on campus "without fear of censorship or negative repercussions." [6]37.5% of Republicans say they feel unsafe on campus.

[7]A recent survey of 1,500 college students by OneClass has found that Republican and Democrat students alike agree on one thing: that Republican students are, in fact, oppressed on campuses across the United States. The survey found that Republicans on college campuses feel unwelcome, afraid, unsafe, secretive, and powerless. The numbers show that both sides know this is a fact.

---

5 www.RISEstudentcoaching.com/resources

6 www.RISEstudentcoaching.com/resources

7 www.RISEstudentcoaching.com/resources

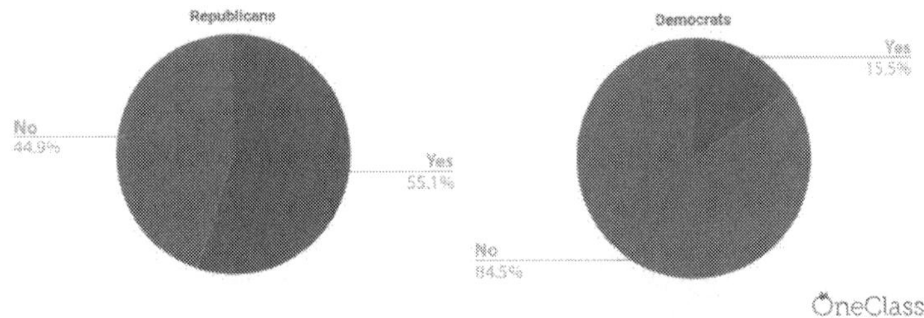
Do you tend to hide your political views from your friends?
Republicans
No
44.9%
Yes
55.1%
Democrats
Yes
15.5%
No
84.5%
OneClass

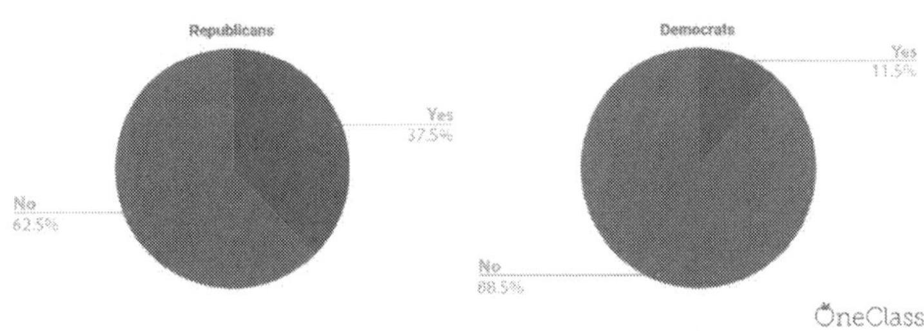
Do you ever feel unsafe on campus for having your political views?
Republicans
Yes
37.5%
No
62.5%
Democrats
Yes
11.5%
No
88.5%
OneClass

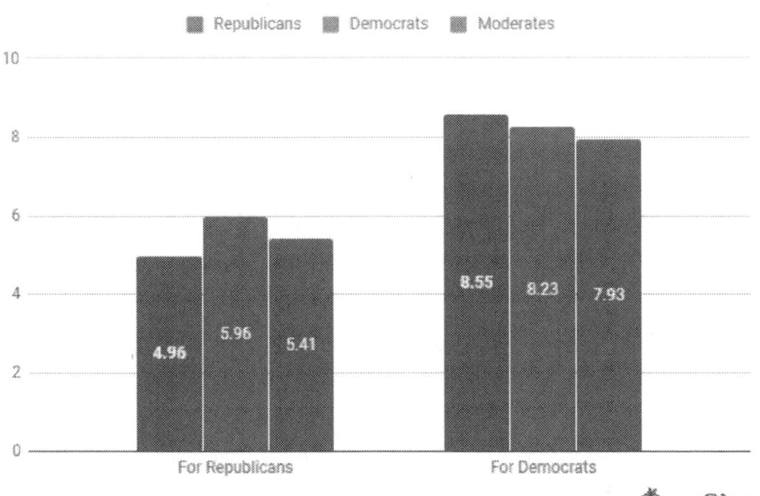
How welcoming is your college campus?
Republicans
Democrats
Moderates
10
8
6
4
2
0
4.96
5.96
5.41
8.55
8.23
7.93
For Republicans
For Democrats
OneClass

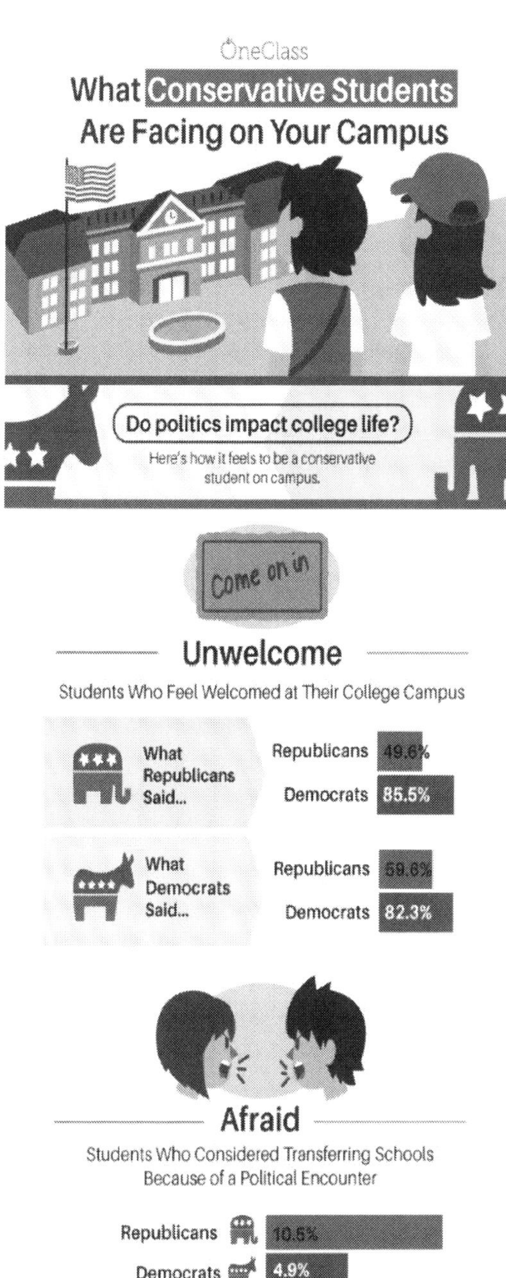
OneClass
What Conservative Students Are Facing on Your Campus
Do politics impact college life?
Here's how it feels to be a conservative student on campus.
Come on in
Unwelcome
Students Who Feel Welcomed at Their College Campus
What Republicans Said...
Republicans 49.6%
Democrats 85.5%
What Democrats Said...
Republicans 59.6%
Democrats 82.3%
Afraid
Students Who Considered Transferring Schools Because of a Political Encounter
Republicans 10.5%
Democrats 4.9%

Unsafe

Students Who Feel Unsafe on Campus Because of Their Political View

Republicans  37.5%

Democrats 11.5%

Secretive

Students Who Hide Their Political Views from Friends

Republicans  55.1%

Democrats  15.5%

Powerless

Student Government Seats Are Politically Biased

What Republicans Said...

39.9% I don't know

33.8% Yes

26.3% No

What Democrats Said...

45.5% I don't know

19.1% Yes

35.4% No

OneClass

Source

https://oneclass.com/blog/uncategorized/146680-what-conservative-students-face-on-your-campus.en.html

Frequently, university administration denies conservative groups the same liberty as liberal groups in bringing outside speakers to campus. Even when allowed, conservative groups are often charged exorbitant 'security fees' after the administration assesses the supposedly high likelihood of a student riot resulting from the presence of non-liberal ideas.

In an April 29, 2023, article published in WND, an attorney for the Alliance Defending Freedom (ADF) describes how the University of Texas at Arlington charged a conservative student organization an unreasonable security fee when a speaker from TPUSA was invited to campus.

[8]"Charging over $28,000 for two small events is prohibitively expensive speech – not free speech," explained lawyer Caleb Dalton in the ADF report on the dispute.

"The University of Texas at Arlington charged TPUSA outrageous security fees for two small campus events simply because of fear about how *others* might react to TPUSA's speech. This is exactly the type of suppression the First Amendment forbids. Implementing such security fees is what's known as a 'heckler's veto,' an action which unconstitutionally allows those who oppose certain speech to censor it simply by protesting or threatening to protest. We urge UTA officials to rescind these unlawful charges quickly and amend their policies to protect every student's freedom of speech."

At the University of Nebraska, Kerney, a state university with a student population of around 6,000 students serving the western half of rural Nebraska, one would assume that the culture surrounding the University would drive the campus culture, thus allowing for unique and diverse learning environments and opportunities across the state's

8 www.RISEstudentcoaching.com/resources

university system. In this case, the representative culture of the Kerney area is traditional, conservative, and Christian.

The campus chapter of Turning Point USA (TPUSA) had enlisted the Governor of Nebraska to speak on campus. This was an achievement for the students to celebrate. They had booked an esteemed speaker to visit their campus! As an educational process, this was an accomplishment to be acknowledged. Students were required to first and foremost work together as a small team, research the request process to submit to the Governor's office, write a proposal and invitation, correspond with the Governor's office and coordinate with campus representatives to book a space and date, and to publicize the event.

From an educator's perspective, this was an accomplishment that one could only hope to replicate in the classroom for credit. However, this wasn't met by officials with nods of approval, accolades or fanfare. The Board of Regents deemed the Governor of Nebraska speaking on a state university campus to be "too controversial." The Board of Regents, along with the university administration, *restricted* publicity of the event. At the last moment, the day before the scheduled event, the students were allowed to issue a press release.

[9]Yet, in a story published in "The Kearney Hub," UNK Chancellor Doug Kristensen said it's rare when the governor visits UNK, so he must have believed the opportunity to speak was worth his time. "Governors have tons and tons of requests. For him to come here is a special event," Kristensen said.

Considering this from a student's point of view, this double-talk and conflicting actions only propagates mistrusts, frustration, and more feelings of disempowerment and disrespect. One can only imagine the thoughts and emotions of those student leaders that worked to host this

9 www.RISEstudentcoaching.com/resources

event when they went home at the end of the day. It is easy to understand why so many students suffer from depression and emotional distress.

These headlines have become all too familiar:

Leftist screams, kicks down table during Turning Point USA event

Left-wing rioters shut down conservative pundit's talk at U. New Mexico

College Republicans allege speaker was restricted due to fear of controversy

[10]A 2021 Foundation for Individual Rights and Expression survey found that 23% of college students believe it is okay to use violence to shut down speech. Recent survey findings revealed that less than half of self-identified conservatives feel welcome on their campus with 38% revealing that they feel *actively unsafe*. Compare this to the 88.5% of self-identified liberals who report feeling safe and at ease.

"Your local conservative isn't a Nazi, and contrary to the popular 'punch a Nazi' slogan that's thrown around campuses, they don't deserve to be abused," stated a current university student when talking about her recent experience hosting a conservative speaker. "It can get scary, especially for a girl. You never know who's watching you, or who will come after you later. We try to stay in groups all the time, but sometimes you can't help being alone. I hate being afraid like this."

Students report horror stories of being verbally attacked and threatened by the people around them. Faculty and staff that speak out or hold contrary beliefs are also fearful. These perceptions of "everyone thinks this way" on college campuses may explain why 72% of Republican college students say the political climate prevents

10 www.RISEstudentcoaching.com/resources

them from saying things they believe because others might find them offensive. About a quarter (26%) of Republican college students feel they can share their political views.

[11]The bias goes beyond what one would assume to be 'conservative.' Thinking that varies from the latest progressive viewpoint is a target to be silenced. Linda Williams Favero interviewed 50 gender studies professors across a range of disciplines, most of whom worked at UK universities, for an article published September 15, 2022, in [12]Times Higher Education.

"Having approached the topic with an open mind... My discussions left me no doubt that a culture of discrimination, silencing and fear has taken hold across the universities in England and many countries beyond," Favero wrote.

Favero found that the gender critical feminist (meaning that they maintain that there is a difference between biological sex) had faced negative repercussions for years for expressing their views.

They are all labeled TERF's or "trans-exclusionary radical feminist." They sometimes say their arguments are "hate speech" or "rhetorical violence" and compare them to fascist or eugenicists.

Among other experiences, Favero's interviewees describe "complaints to and by management, attempts to shut down events, no platforming, disinvitations, intimidation, smears, and losing career progression opportunities, including being blocked from jobs," Favero wrote. Others told her of being "physically removed from events" and experiencing massive online abuse, including incitement to murder.

---

11 www.RISEstudentcoaching.com/resources

12 www.RISEstudentcoaching.com/resources

[13]Chico State College Republicans President Michael Curry told The College Fix, "Over the last semester myself and the members of the Chico State Republicans have been spat on, battered, assaulted, followed around campus, sexually harassed, and even mobbed by 300 students at once. This is the kind of environment that has been created by the modern day college campus."

[14]In a recent interview, one student from the University of Portland conveyed his experience, "I'm kind of gagged if you know what I mean, because the liberal students here are able to say everything that they want to because they are in the majority, but for me who's in the minority, if I try to say anything, I will face instant backlash. They don't even let me finish my sentences.

"I feel like if I transferred I would be able to have true debates in class instead of just one-sided," he said. "The debates here aren't much of a debate because the people on the left keep shutting me up."

On the campus of the University of Minnesota, for example, conservative students say, "Free speech is being shut down," adding that they have been threatened with violence and attacked on social media.

Many add that protestors are trying to label anyone with a conservative ideology as a neo-Nazi, white supremacist or alt-right extremist spewing hate speech.

[15]Republicans are two times more likely to want to transfer schools after a political encounter than Liberals. The pressure that comes from not fitting in, from being labeled racist, misogynist, and a bigot is too much for most students to handle. They are leaving to find a

13 www.RISEstudentcoaching.com/resources

14 www.RISEstudentcoaching.com/resources

15 www.RISEstudentcoaching.com/resources

better environment; a more welcoming campus. Oftentimes they're wrong. Campuses are overwhelmingly liberal regardless of seemingly philosophical alliances such as a Christian University or an Ivy League school. Even rural Colleges and Universities or traditional conservative campuses are pressured into "woke" philosophies.

The culture of intolerance on university campuses is undeniable. There exists a large irony in the fact that liberals tend to tout themselves as the political identity of tolerance, yet 55% of conservative students are so afraid of backlash for their political ideas that they masquerade as liberal.

Ashley, a student on a large southern campus, was working with a conservative group to host a speaker discussing current events and public policy. The student group followed the policies and procedures for approval including a synopsis of the presentation, which was deemed appropriate and non-controversial by university officials. The speaker was approved, but no other accommodations for safety and security were made.

The day of the event, as Ashley was assisting with set up and preparations for the speaker, a group of students gathered around her and started chanting, "f*** you, f** you, go home!"

Ashley recalled, "And nothing was done to those students! They were protesting a simple speaker! It was public bullying and nothing was done! The university stood by and watched that happen!"

Although colleges have strong bullying policies, including bystander reporting policies, the consequences are not significant enough to students to report the bullying of their conservative peers. It seems an obvious assumption that bullying is only defined as harmful when it is a subject that is not conservative.

In another incident, Bryce, a student that was hosting a conservative speaker, was threatened by the president of the Democratic Socialist Club. He threatened he would beat up Bryce personally if he continued hosting speakers and working with the conservative organization Turning Point USA. Bryce reported him to the administration. Nothing was ever done, to Bryce's knowledge. "If another student had threatened publicly to beat another student over their opinion, over anything, they would immediately be sent to student conduct and most likely be suspended, expelled, or at the least suffer sanctions," Bryce expressed.

Overall enrollment shifts happen constantly. The shift that's currently occurring is concerning those in higher education. Data shows enrollment for white male students is declining.

[16]Cumulatively, male enrollment decline during the pandemic is now -9.3%, four percentage points steeper than the female decline of -5.3%, over the two years from 2019 to 2021.

[17]As explained in Inside Higher Ed, "One of the most common annual refrains I have heard in my decades on the faculty and in administration in higher education has been 'Let's increase the freshman class by 10 percent next fall!'"

Motivated by the need to generate more tuition and housing money, universities have looked to increase the on-campus undergraduate student base. The prospects of such increases are looking dimmer as the "demographic cliff" anticipated by up to a 15 percent drop in freshman prospects approaches beginning in 2025 due to the decline in birth rate in the 2008 recession and lasting for years after. Those missing babies in 2008 would have begun entering college 17 years later, in 2025.

16 www.RISEstudentcoaching.com/resources

17 www.RISEstudentcoaching.com/resources

Colleges are worried about the enrollment "cliff" that's anticipated beginning in 2025.

These drops come in the context of a half a dozen years of annual declines in births in the United States. Yet the birth rate is not the only trend threatening higher education as we know it today. There are mounting factors that dissuade prospective students from making a large investment in degrees and instead choosing to go with online alternatives to traditional higher education.

[18]Speaking with The Financial Times, Kirill Pyshkin, senior portfolio manager at Credit Suisse, likened the disruption to what happened in the film industry a few years ago: "This is education's Netflix moment." Sean Gallagher, an executive professor of education policy at Northeastern University and founder of Northeastern's Center for the Future of Higher Education and Talent Strategy, agrees: "This looks to be a catalytic moment. Like what's happened with the rapid digitization of so many other areas of our daily lives, we've probably gained in a few months a level of interest and participation in online education that would have steadily played out over years.

"Meanwhile, Coursera, the large-scale for-profit online degree, certificate and course provider has posted its earnings from the first quarter. Last year, Coursera reported 70 million learners with more than 200 partners. This year, profits are up more than 70 percent over the first quarter last year, to some $50 million. Meanwhile, Google has announced its massive new Career Certificates in an array of fields, with costs starting at as little as $39 per month. Microsoft and, of course, LinkedIn also are leading providers of professional certifications."

Lastly, Mr. Pyshkin states, "a Strada Education Network COVID-19 Work and Education Survey found that one in four Americans plan to

18 www.RISEstudentcoaching.com/resources

enroll in an education program in the next six months, and they also expressed a preference for non degree programs, skills training and online options. Workers are not the only ones expressing little interest in four-year degree programs. Increasing numbers of CEOs are dropping the baccalaureate from a requirement for hiring."

Competition is rapidly growing; the pool of "traditional" students is evaporating; employers are dropping degree requirements; and, with student debt now surpassing $1.7 trillion, students are looking for more cost-effective paths to the knowledge and skills they seek. "The fundamental business model for delivering education is broken," said Rick Beyer, a senior fellow and practice area lead for mergers and affiliations at the Association of Governing Boards of Universities and Colleges. "The consolidation era started a few years ago. It will continue. We will see more closures."

Clamoring for enrollment, all institutions of higher education are pursuing students of marginalized groups often at the expense of their own constituency. A public university in a rural state that's funded by taxpayer dollars is desperately recruiting students of color. The "why" is a multi-faceted answer, but the rule of business prevails - "follow the money." The higher percentage of marginalized groups, the more federal and state dollars they're taking in. Institutions are categorized according to their enrollment statistics. The goal of this university is to move from a PWI (PRIMARILY WHITE INSTITUTION), to an HSI (HISPANIC SERVICE INSTITUTION). What is talked about behind the scenes (and never talked about in public) is that the objective in these rural state institutions is to retain students of color at a higher percentage than the demographics of their state population.

In Fall 2020, about 4.2 million students were enrolled at Hispanic-serving institutions (HSIs).

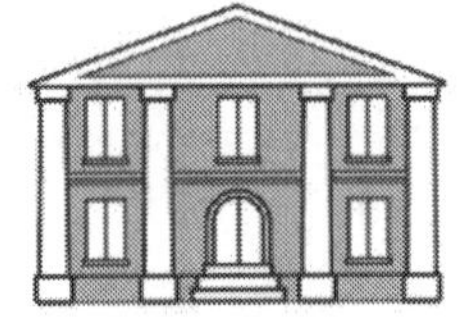

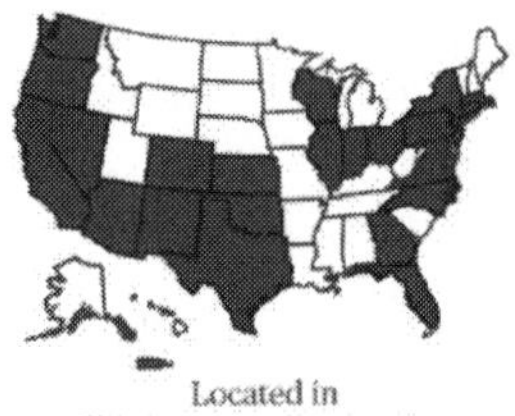

2,044,530 Hispanic students enrolled at HSIs

451 Hispanic-serving institutions

Located in 24 states and Puerto Rico

SOURCE: U.S. Department of Education, National Center for Education Statistics, Integrated Postsecondary Education Data System (IPEDS), Spring 2021, Fall Enrollment component; and Office of Postsecondary Education, 2021 Eligibility Matrix, retrieved December 2, 2021, from https://www2.ed.gov/about/offices/list/ope/idues/eligibility.html.

[19]Institutions of higher learning are regularly identified in scholarship and conversation by their racial composition, which generally reflects a distinction between predominantly white institutions (PWIs), and minority-serving institutions (MSIs). While PWI is not an official designation for any institution in the United States, six categories of MSIs are classified by the Higher Education Act: Hispanic Serving Institutions (HSIs), Historically Black Colleges and Universities (HBCUs), Tribal Colleges and Universities (TCUs), Alaska Native Serving Institutions (ANSIs), Native Hawaiian Serving Institutions (NHSIs), and a general category of Minority Serving Institutions (MSIs). The purpose of this article is to critically examine the term "predominantly white institution." The premise is that what is predominant at these institutions stems from much more than simple numbers of white students as compared to numbers of students from underrepresented racial groups. Patterns of representation are examined through a lens of critical race theory (CRT).[20]

19 www.RISEstudentcoaching.com/resources

20 www.RISEstudentcoaching.com/resources

That was never the intention of the state university system. Serving the children of those communities was the purpose of a decentralized state university system. The metrics that used to quantify the demographics of the student enrollment are skewed to produce numbers that are advantageous to the institution's needs at the time - which is always money.

It's a wonder students get an education at all. For a period of about three years, international students were viewed as a cash cow. Departments were invented, staff hired, budgets bulged, and enrollment requirements conformed to the money roll at the time. International recruiters were lauded for their admirable achievements enticing foreign students to their university. Once there, however, challenges overwhelmed the system. There were cultural divides, language barriers, and classrooms filled with students requiring special consideration and adaptations.

With institutions chasing the money and swaying with the wind, who stands for the students?

Are the students learning or developing? Are *they* the institution's primary concern? Educating students is their primary responsibility, but one that's being neglected, and parents are literally paying the price.

Rural students find this racial bias, including language commonly used by their own university, such as underprivileged or disadvantaged, especially insulting. Rural students had few of the privileges that are associated with "white privilege." They are in the barn milking cows at 4:00 AM, picking corn until well after midnight, "pulling calves" in snow and rainstorms, and "cleaning barn" throughout the summer.

The university system no longer prioritizes the local students who aren't bringing in the federal dollars that are reserved for students that qualify for programs designated for students of color.

Bias begins at the institutional level on every campus, regardless of the purport that it's 'grassroots' being initiated by the students. Even conservative appearing private campuses are as functionally progressive as public colleges and universities. The back-door motivation of gaining state and federal dollars drives campuses to reinvent their campus into an environment for underprivileged students and students of color. They have instituted the culture shift from the traditional collegiate atmosphere to progressive bastions of wokeness. They have sold every parent's dream of their child experiencing the traditional 'campus life' that they knew as a young adult to the highest bidder; the government dollar.

How deep is the relationship between the federal government and higher education? "Follow the money" applies to funding as well as implanting progressive ideology into campus culture.

[21]An example of this was revealed in a May 25, 2023 BPR article.

"Documents obtained via Freedom of Information Act (FOIA) requests by conservative watchdog group, the Media Research Center (MRC), and shared with Fox News Digital[22], reveal that the DHS's Targeted Violence and Terrorism Prevention Grant Program (TVTP) awarded $352,109 to the University of Dayton for its PREVENTS-OH program.

"According to its website[23], the PREVENTS-OH program "aims to develop a proactive, informed and resilient network of organizations, coalitions and civic entities aware and capable of collaborating to prevent domestic violent extremism in Southwest Ohio."

21 www.RISEstudentcoaching.com/resources

22 www.RISEstudentcoaching.com/resources

23 www.RISEstudentcoaching.com/resources

"The money was granted to 'draw on the expertise of the University of Dayton faculty'" to fight 'domestic violence extremism and hate movements,'" Fox News Digital reports.

"Featured on the university's grant application to the DHS was a footnote that linked to a Dayton conference where the "Pyramid of Far-Right Radicalization" was presented.

"At the base of the pyramid was Fox News, the Christian Broadcasting Network, the Republican Party, the American Conservative Union Foundation, The Heritage Foundation, Tea Party Patriots, the John Birch Society, and the NRA.

"Going up a step, the pyramid features, among others, Breitbart News, the Make America Great Again (MAGA) movement, PragerUniversity, Turning Point USA, and the pro-police Blue Lives Matter movement.

"This terrorism task force is engaged in an active effort to demonize and eliminate Christian, conservative, and Republican organizations using federal taxpayer dollars," Brent Bozell, founder and president of the Media Research Center, told Fox News Digital. "What we have uncovered calls for criminal prosecution. The American people need to know those who are abusing their positions in the federal government will be held accountable for their criminal behavior."

Reports Fox News Digital: "In 2021, the University of Dayton held a seminar called 'Extremism, Rhetoric, and Democratic Precarity' featuring several experts on extremism who compared mainstream conservatives to genocidal extremists."

[24]"A genocide expert from Rutgers University compared at the seminar the Trump administration to Pol Pot's Khmer Rouge which killed roughly 1.5 – 2 million Cambodians in the 1970s."

Organized and intentional programs that are aimed to discredit and disparage conservatives and Christians on university campuses are funded by our own federal government, and the universities are complicit in the scheme! Their targets are you and your children. The opponents that we face are well funded, influential, and powerful. It's imperative that we stand together and face them by voicing our truth.

Leah's story illustrates the level of contempt the institution has for faculty that *just might* be conservative, and the power that liberal students hold.

Leah was hired as an instructor at a large upper midwestern university. Being her first job teaching at the Collegiate level, the challenge was exciting and the experience was exceptionally rewarding. Acknowledging the inevitable learning curve she faced, she embraced

24 www.RISEstudentcoaching.com/resources

the challenge and developed relationships with the faculty in her department, regarding them as mentors. Having earned her Ph.D., she found herself working her way up to her dream teaching job; being a tenured faculty at a prestigious university. Over a period of three years, she gained experience and insight into the competencies and skill of teaching at the university level.

Each semester, evaluations are completed by the students at the conclusion of the course. The majority of students' scores reflected her professionalism and dedication to her students. It's expected that the displeased students use the opportunity to provide their feedback as well. The outstanding evaluations were peppered with a handful of lower ratings which she earnestly studied to extract the constructive criticism that she could implement for improvement.

One semester started with an immediate disconnect with a student. He had instantly labeled her as a conservative simply because her curriculum encouraged a range of thought and ideas. It was his expectation that the content of any course, and the only narrative that was acceptable, was that of progressive liberals. Each time an assignment was given for a reading or project that required them to research or reflect on a variety of points of view, he contentiously complained. Throughout the semester his aggressiveness escalated. The student finally reported her to the Dean alleging discrimination. Although an investigation was conducted, only the reporting student and a handful of students in the class that supported him were interviewed. No other professors who had experienced similar difficulties working with him were contacted, nor were the students in the class that had spoken to Leah throughout the semester that they felt intimidated, bullied, and manipulated during class by this student and his friends.

The conclusion of the investigation was not officially communicated to Leah. She simply received an unexpected email informing her that her contract would not be renewed for the upcoming year. Leah was terminated by her University because she expected her students to think beyond liberal narratives and assumptions. She expected students to learn and to think on their own as independent individuals. Leah's expectations were that of a scholar educating students how to be scholars. And for that she was unfairly terminated.

This is the fear of conservative faculty throughout the U.S. It's very real. They see this happen around them. They know the consequences that befall the brave faculty and instructors with professional integrity that dare to offer a curriculum that is simply neutral, factual, and not progressive or "woke." Faculty are required to go along to get along to preserve their professional status and ultimately their job. To remain loyal to their morals, values, and professionalism, they risk losing their position, their benefits, their means to support their family on the whim of liberal administrators.

For many parents, it's overwhelming to figure out where to start. You've already taken the first and most important step by becoming informed and raising your awareness to the reality of the progressive campus culture. Your willingness to take action is next. Suggestions are offered in later chapters to reinforce your ability to set in motion actionable strategies to support your student. The RISE (Resilience And Independence Skills for Engagement) Student Coaching program, detailed in Chapter 6, offers parents a coach with expertise in skill building programming that's tailored to your student's strengths and developmental needs. The RISE Student Coaching program also offers peer support to ensure that every student has access to like-minded contemporaries at campuses across the country.

ACADEMIC BIAS

Slogging to class, the crisp autumn breeze was nudging him awake. It'd been a long night watching the election results come in. A handful of friends and James had gathered to eat pizza and celebrate that their candidate, Trump, won the presidential election. Trump was really a strange guy; he wasn't what James pictured when he thought of a US President, but his values and beliefs aligned with James and his family's so he was a supporter. Tired, but happy, James trudged up the stairs of North Hall for his first class of the day, Physiology.

James was a sophomore and had just declared his kinesiology major. Thrilled to have decided on a career path, he looked forward to connecting with others in the program. His T.A. was a pretty cool guy and he'd secretly hoped they would become friends next semester.

The building was unusually quiet. Entering his classroom, James was greeted at the door by his T.A. He was offered a QR code to scan. Looking up, James asked if the code was for a study guide. No, he was told. It was a resource guide for the campus community that was grieving the loss of the Presidential election. There were support and grief groups, 1-1 counseling sessions, and a suicide hotline number. James blinked and looked at the code in astonishment. He looked up and told the T.A. that he supported Trump and was glad he'd won. The T.A. stood upright and recited a laundry list of accusations against James' character. He was accused of believing in every extreme right-wing viewpoint, including being racist, a white supremacist, misogynist, homophobic, and a crazy judgmental Christian.

Stunned, James tried to collect his thoughts. He was fiscally conservative, but not really socially conservative. How could he ever explain all of this standing in the doorway when his class was about to start?

Weeks later, the effects of the election had taken its toll on his campus. Students were more fractured than ever. Hate speech (against Trump and Trump supporters) was vile, violent, and very public. James and his friends were offered no forum or platform by campus to communicate their views. They knew to remain silent, knowing that they were being unfairly judged and stereotyped. Nobody cared, though.

In the classroom, students fear the possible backlash to their political views. Students report that they have lied on assignments to make themselves sound more liberal. They believe that sounding "too conservative" might affect their relationship with the professor and even their grade.

A professor shared, "Students came to me requesting a closed door meeting. They were complaining that an entire composition class was about Trump, climate change, and Racism. Feeling responsible to advocate for these students, I went to the Dean.

"I asked, 'Do you really believe that this is really OK?' The Dean backed the faculty citing academic freedom.

"I asked specifically about a book they are required to read, 'Just Us,' by Caludia Rankine.

"The Dean went on, 'They (the faculty) can choose the books they want. It's their unrestricted academic freedom.'

"The irony for me is that another professor can require 'Just Us,' but I can't require 'Hillbilly Elegy,'" by JD Vance. It's too conservative!

"What is it like for the students that have to sit there? What are they thinking about themselves? Especially the white males that are targeted in this genre of writing; in this cultural philosophy?

I never thought I'd live to see the day that students would sit in classes and be shamed for the color of their skin. No one will do anything under the guise of academic freedom.

"In an Anthropology course, half the class curriculum is dedicated to white privilege with the explicit goal that the 'country will change to make up for the sins on white people.'

"The courses that are the most impregnated with Critical Race Theory are the social sciences, such as Psychology and Sociology, and English, Literature, and Composition. Nearly all faculty, however, conduct their classes through a far-left lens, requiring students to state their preferred pronouns, and affirm their white privilege in class discussions and assignments.

"A white male student told me that he was so traumatized by being forced to listen to a far-leftist professor every day 'dedicating class to bashing white people' that he dropped the class.

"He said, 'I'm so worried for you, that a student is going to "Report" you. You'll get in so much trouble.' His worry was that it would 'get out' that I love my country. I would be rated poorly by other students on "RateMy Professor.com" and by faculty during my peer review. He nominated me for a teaching award, but privately told me, 'I know you won't win because you're a red fish swimming in a blue ocean.'"

Current required reading for college courses, this review of "Just Us," by Claudia Rankine, writing for the Washington Independent Review of Books, is a brilliant summary of the book:

> [25]*In "Ethical Loneliness," Rankine tells on a white friend who attended a Black-authored play with her but refused to budge when a character called for white people in the audience*

25 www.RISEstudentcoaching.com/resources

to get up on stage. Rankine's friend stayed put, which made Rankine feel "tense," "resentful," and "betrayed." Rankine found it "unbearable." But the friend doubled down and later explained: "I sometimes shrink from scenes where I'm asked, personally or generally, to feel bad as a white person — where whatever else is being asked, I'm being asked to feel shame, guilt, to do penance, to stand corrected, to sit down chastised...I feel like unholy transactions are in the offing, like white moral masochism is getting a thrill."

It is there, more than 200 pages into Just Us, that I become (ironically) clear: The book seems to be for people in need of that feeling of guilt.

The book's title makes it seem like it might be about grittier struggles, though. Just Us gets its name from a famous Pryor/ Mooney quote about the prison industrial complex: "When you go down to the courthouse you look for justice, but you find just us." But Rankine's book feels far removed from survival-level struggle and grotesque Americanisms like mass incarceration.

Thus, the nod to Pryor's work seems unfair. Just Us is not a book about Black women shot down by the police in their homes or incarcerated for minor crimes. It's about Black women who enter the country club through the front door. Rankine's 360-page exposé of microaggression feels far from whatever strengthens its author. But it may be purposefully so.

[26]If campus conservatives don't believe they have the numbers stacked against them, at least they ought to know the political makeup

26 www.RISEstudentcoaching.com/resources

of college professors: Democratic professors outnumber Republican professors 10 to 1. Digging deeper, research has shown 52% of students have said their professors or course instructors express their own unrelated social or political beliefs "often" in class. [27]One student stated, "I basically haven't been able to say anything towards my beliefs in two years here. And I'm not kidding. I'm not exaggerating."

[28]In an interview with The Beacon, Madison Wagner states, "Unfortunately, I think a lot of people, especially in our generation, hear the word Republican and they think 'You are a terrible person.' I've had people say that to me before. Like 'Oh you're conservative? You're an asshole.' Or when they think you are a Republican on everything. And that is so not the case."

[29]Similar patterns are seen in assessments of the climate for "liberals" and "conservatives" in the country, with clear majorities of Republicans – including 72% of conservative Republicans – saying liberals in the country are very comfortable to freely and openly express their political views, while just 14% say conservatives in the country are very comfortable to do this. In comparison, 54% of liberal Democrats think conservatives are very comfortable freely and openly expressing their political views, and just 34% say this about liberals.[30]

---

27 www.RISEstudentcoaching.com/resources

28 www.RISEstudentcoaching.com/resources

29 www.RISEstudentcoaching.com/resources

30 www.RISEstudentcoaching.com/resources

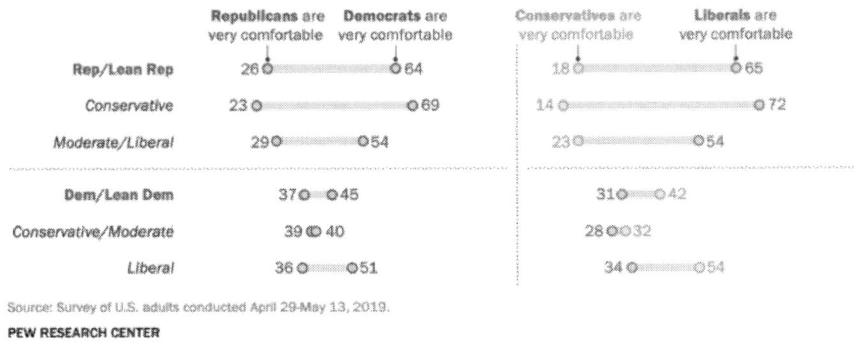

There is a culture of intolerance on university campuses. Precisely there lies the inexcusable irony in the fact that liberals tend to tout themselves as the political identity of tolerance, yet in their best stronghold (higher education), 55% of conservative students are so afraid of backlash for their political ideas that they masquerade as liberal.

[31]A narrative study used the spiral of silence to understand conservative student experiences in a teacher education program[32] (Journell, 2017). Findings revealed conservative students would spiral into silence after they observed their classmates' words and actions[33](Journell, 2017). The author also explained how conservative students "perceived hostility" and experienced "backlash" from their liberal peers (p. 120), and how a double standard existed in the social justice focused program. A sociopolitical identity is an important factor in how one evaluates and experiences their environment.

31 www.RISEstudentcoaching.com/resources

32 www.RISEstudentcoaching.com/resources

33 www.RISEstudentcoaching.com/resources

Playing the game of "parrot" feels like the only way some students survived an English Composition class. Professors have given the feedback, "You haven't appropriately learned the class material" when students have turned in composition assignments that were of opposing political views, or the color of their skin was not deserving of the content they wrote.

Alexis' feedback from her professor was commentary of her 'person' and not her writing. She had submitted a fiction writing assignment in which she incorporated a personal struggle of her own. Having been overweight her entire life, she knew deeply the agony of judgment of others and low self-esteem. In the science fiction genre, she explored her experience by, at times, comparing it with the experience of the trans struggle to fit into society. Inquiring about her low score, the professor said, "Afterall, you *are* a privileged, white female who just has a bit of a problem. Writing, comparing your "personhood" to another, is problematic when you are generally more privileged than others."

"The professor thought the story was offensive because I was telling a story about a condition that in our society is considered an outgroup. I was told that I'm a white privileged girl and I don't have a right to tell the *professor* to 'F off' in her class like this. I didn't know what to do. I acquiesced. I rewrote the story. She was mad. In the story I compared my condition, being overweight, with being trans in today's society. It's another example of being an outsider; being something that you can't control and only you know on the inside what that feels like looking out into the world.

"I didn't disagree with trans people's plight or rights. I didn't say that I felt trans was bad or wrong or that it didn't exist. In fact, my story validated trans people! It validated that trans people have a condition that they can't control or change. They are simply trying to fit into the world around them and that was the comparison I was making to another condition. I was judged based upon my skin color and told I had no right to write this story. I was so mad that I had to take trans out of the story. I even cried. She bullies everyone in her class. Everyone has to believe what she believes or we are under the scrutiny and the threat of failing. I was told to make the *right* choice and to change it to not be offensive!"

This is how composition is being taught at major universities today. It is not based on academic rubrics, but on the opinion of the student by the faculty member and not their abilities or scholastic achievements. The faculty hold all of the power and it's their way or the highway.

In a Freshman seminar called "White Privilege," a group discussion regarding the 'astonishing disparate advantages' that whites have in this country left students speechless. Their first class, their first semester of college, their first week away from home, they were required to confront the entire country's history of racism and their personal participation in it. Seventeen and eighteen year olds may have a persona that projects confidence and a boisterous nature, but all of them are still children developing into young adults. Their malleable identity is a work of art, awaiting its next stage of unfolding. Any adult that is in tune with teens, much less an educator with an advanced degree, understands the ebb and flow of their unique evolution. One with authority will facilitate their unfolding rather than manipulating them into compliance. The consequence of this professor's approach produces the opposite of their intended outcome. Alexis tuned out of her writing class for the rest of the course, and fashioned a personal mental shield to protect her throughout her entire college experience. Entering academia for the first time, students quickly learn that they are not valued or respected, and their apology for their 'personhood' must precede them into the classroom.

A white male student attending a "Family Studies" sociology class was told that white men are toxic and are detrimental to the development of their own (yet unborn) children. The professor ensured that each male student assimilated that belief system through her coursework by assigning projects and research papers that supported this sole belief system. Meeting privately throughout the semester, some of the young men validated their masculinity, and the value of it in a family. They all agreed, however, that as a privileged white male, their presence or opinion did not matter to the instructor, and they would all 'go along' to get the grade, regardless of their personal humiliation.

In a *political tolerance class*, students were instructed to write a paper on the state of the Republican party in today's politics – but were only allowed to use sources from a provided list and had to write a paper that was supported by the professor's sources. This list included only opinion articles of the farthest left political bent, painting all conservatives as racist, heartless, greedy monsters.

[34]No one can beg away from this phenomenon. It affects every taxpayer in the US. Whether one agrees with the philosophical trends of the day or not, the direct financial burden of social justice general education requirements is at least $10 billion a year nationwide — and rising fast — according to a report released by the National Association of Scholars.

[35]Just because 82 percent of faculty identify as liberal while only one percent of professors call themselves conservatives does not mean there is a problem with bias on campus, according to The Harvard Crimson. The Crimson editors commented on their own survey which found an overwhelming majority of professors classify themselves as "liberal" or "very liberal."

34 www.RISEstudentcoaching.com/resources

35 www.RISEstudentcoaching.com/resources

While the board wrote that while it did favor "debate and discourse" which are "central to a vibrant intellectual community" and the "lifeblood of academia," that does not mean that the campus needs more conservative professors.

[36]According to research from the Pew Research Center, liberals are more likely to unfriend you over politics - online and offline. It shows Republicans and Democrats share very different social lives on campus. Republicans have to suppress their voice to feel accepted, while the Democrats can speak without thinking twice. If campus conservatives didn't believe they had the numbers stacked against them, at least they ought to know the political makeup of college professors: Democratic professors outnumber Republican professors 10 to 1.

Digging deeper, research has shown 52% of students have said their professors or course instructors express their own unrelated social or political beliefs "often" in class. For conservative students, it would be unwise to believe their professors wouldn't let their political preference affect their grading.

There is a widespread perception that most faculty and students at American colleges and universities are liberal. But it's not just perception. Empirical studies of faculty ideology confirm what most students observe. About 12% of professors are conservative while about 60% are liberal. Further, nearly half (46%) of current college and graduate students identify as Democrats or independents who lean Democratic. About a quarter identify as Republican (27%).

[37]Democratic and Republican students see their college campuses very differently. A majority (59%) of Republican college students believe that most faculty members are liberal. In contrast, only 35%

36 www.RISEstudentcoaching.com/resources

37 www.RISEstudentcoaching.com/resources

of Democratic college students agree most professors are liberal. Democratic students are also about twice as likely as Republican students to think their professors are moderate (32% vs. 16%) or conservative (14% vs. 9%).

[38]"The class is just an echo chamber of people parroting what the professor believes, rather than anyone actively engaging the material," one student wrote. "But I feel like I'm the only one to notice or be uncomfortable by this lack of discourse, so I keep quiet."

Several students that I interviewed for this book used the same phrase, "parroting," to describe their classroom experience. That is not why parents pay high tuition rates, or society depends upon educated young adults to lead us into the future. But it is what the progressives rely on. Students become passive "parrots" in the place of learning to become engaged thinkers and speakers.

There is an assumption that people think the way they do. Reporting on his experience, one student said, "If people were to accept that there are differing views on campus, that would be kind of nice." Last semester he had a theology Professor who is very liberal, so he chose not to bring up his views out of *respect* for the professor.

Victoria, a college senior, reports that she dreads her classes. "I want to tear out my hair because they won't just tell us the facts. Everything is a story. Everything is fiction. We have no facts to base our learning on.

"We were required to read a story about an African-American woman. What I got out of the story is that no one understands her. White women don't understand black women. And all white people are bad. That was what the book portrayed and that was entirely what

38 www.RISEstudentcoaching.com/resources

class discussions were based on. Every discussion surrounded that topic, and that's all. That's the lesson and what the class walked away with. There was no room for any other commentary opinions or even worse, questions. Wouldn't the outcome of literature - of reading a book - be learning and discussing and talking about the concepts and the reasoning and the intent?

"What are we learning? Extra ideas outside the instructor's, or even questions, are simply not allowed. One student with a disability, an obvious physical disability, tried to engage in a conversation and to relate by talking about the feeling of being ostracized in a society where she's a minority and a marginalized person in terms of ability. The professor's reaction was totally overblown! The professor shamed this student in front of the entire class by saying, 'You have privilege because you're white! You cannot sit here and talk about anything having to do with the black experience.'

"The student tried to explain, 'I'm not talking about a black experience. I'm talking about the experience of being a marginalized group. That is something that many people have in common and we could work toward a positive solution for everyone and a better way to get along in the world.'

"The professor repeated that she only wanted to hear from African-American students! No student with a 'white face' under any circumstances could speak to the content of the curriculum, and the book that had been taught."

The white voices were completely silenced. No one was allowed to talk in class or they would be belittled and shamed. Everyone knew it wasn't a safe place to talk about unapproved subjects so the class became more and more silent as the semester went on. Politics were the most important thing in the classroom. More important than course content and more important than student learning. The most important thing to that professor was using a college course as a platform to push her political agenda. She said that her goal for the class was for the students in the class to be anti-racist. No discussion, no other learning, only to be anti-racist. Parents pay tuition, and students incur enormous student debt to be indoctrinated into a value system and to recalibrate their moral compass at the whim of any professor that is at the front of the classroom.

Britt, a freshman student, shared, “I have class with a very woke professor with an anti-racist agenda. I transferred into this school from another one, so my experience is of two different universities. This classroom is so unhealthy. It’s the most unhealthy classroom I’ve ever been in in my life. The bias is so bad I need to be so careful of everything I say. I’m a proud conservative. It took me a long time to grow into acceptance that that’s what I am. I realized that the other things that were being taught and said around campus made me mad. They upset me and I wasn’t sure why, but it’s because I was being told that this was the only right thing to believe. My anger just kept growing. I was feeling like I didn’t even want to go to the dining hall with my friends because I knew that conversations would come back to some liberal topic. I finally just quit eating. I lost 20 pounds because I was avoiding going to the dining hall where I was forced to sit at a table with people that always needed to talk about their classes and all of the things that they were learning that day. It made me sick to my stomach. I couldn’t eat. I had no appetite. I just felt so bad about myself and my family, my home, and my friends. I felt bad about what I had learned in church. I just wanted to stay in my room by myself.

“The professor in my creative writing class didn’t even cover the course objectives. All he wanted to talk about was just his racist opinions against the white students and white people in general. White people are bad and that's all they wanted to talk about.

"I want to transfer back to my old campus. It's funny. It makes me laugh that they were so conservative at my old campus that I felt like I didn't fit in. I wanted to go to another campus so I could fit in with my "liberal" views. And now I hear that my old campus is embracing 'woke' as bad as this one. I don't know where I'll ever fit in. I don't want to transfer again. Every time I transfer I lose credits and I lose time toward graduation.

"The classes are so tense, everyone understands they can't talk. So many students are so afraid to raise their hand, they try to be invisible. You can see students in their chairs just sinking down, putting their heads down, not looking up, just sitting there for the whole class time enduring it.

"In the last year it's gotten so bad so fast. I don't know what's going on. Administration has to be telling them to be political or something, and they must be pushing them really hard. I don't know how normal teachers have gotten this way! Who's telling them to do this? Who's brainwashing them and convincing them that this agenda is more important than the students in their classroom; more important than education? If parents knew that their money was being spent this way so many would be so angry. But students are in a tough situation. If they really tell their parents what's going on in their classes, the parents are probably going to tell them they can't go to school anymore and everyone wants a degree. So students suffer in silence. They sit in classes and look at their phones and leave after class to go to their rooms at the end of the day and feel really bad about themselves.

"They look at the assignments they have in front of them which, by the way, are very different from the assignments that are in the syllabus or the course outline, and they struggle just wondering how they're going to start. What are they going to say that will appease the teacher and will earn them a decent grade? Professors are so irrational now. It's impossible to even have a conversation with them unless you're repeating the gibberish that they tell us in class. I try not to throw a tantrum, but I'm so frustrated and angry all the time.

"Thursdays! I dread Thursdays! I dread my Thursday class all day! I feel anxious just thinking about the class. I feel so crappy and depressed. I sit in class quietly and let the professor walk all over me trying to decide what I could do or say. All I can think about is how fed up I am. I want to stand up and speak out. I do sometimes. It was so much worse inside me when I didn't ever speak up. So often I want to just say, 'can we avoid talking about politics right now?' or, 'I don't agree with that,' but I can't.

"In my class, two students tried to have a discussion about J.K. Rowling and the controversy around her anti-trans statements. The professor made it clear after the conversation started that no point of view would be tolerated in the class that was not opposing J.K. Rowling or vilifying her. For me, she was a role model because she writes so well and I love her stories. I wanted to raise my hand but I was too scared they would look at me and think that I hated trans people, too. I felt ashamed that I liked an author that was perceived as anti-trans. I didn't know what to do. I felt so bad and conflicted for days afterward. When I went back to the next class, I decided I had to speak up. I asked the professor, is this a safe space; that I needed to know. The professor said 'why of course it is.' So I started out explaining that in my opinion, J.K. Rowling is not a bad person and that she's a great writer. She's a great storyteller and that she should be appreciated for her literary contributions, not her political beliefs. I felt I needed to state, too, that I don't dislike trans people personally. I really don't care if someone's trans. I said this is my opinion. The instructor didn't say anything back to me. After class so many students came up to me and said, 'Oh my gosh I feel the same way, I'm so glad you spoke up.'"

Professors are giving assignments that are specifically geared for Liberal outcomes. For example, students in a class were required to volunteer in the community for service hours. They were told to volunteer for a specific number of hours anywhere in the community - except an organization that was a pro-life health clinic. They were allowed to volunteer in a Planned Parenthood or pro-abortion clinic or other non-profit facilities and offices but not the pro-life clinic. They were forbidden to work in the pro-life center and would not get credit for those hours.

The pressure to conform is even greater at the graduate level. Students are avoiding applying to masters level and Ph.D. programs for fear that they will be rejected for their political positions rather than their academic or personal achievements.

Turning Point USA is a conservative organization that supports and educates young people about the importance of limited government, free markets, and free speech. Leadership in a national organization would typically be an advantageous affiliation to list on a graduate school application. Jesse, a conservative student planning to apply to dental school programs, rejected a leadership position in TPUSA because he thought it would reflect badly on his character from the perspective of the graduate admissions committee. Jesse believes that conservative students are rejected at a higher percentage than liberal candidates, and he didn't want to compromise his strong graduate application with a public conservative affiliation.

STUDENT AFFAIRS BIAS

Gisele', a Freshman university student, and a black conservative Christian immigrant from Zambia, found herself shunned by her peers after her first week in the dorms.

Gisele's parents immigrated to the US when she was 10. She completed grade school, middle and high school in her local community, a suburb of Kansas City. Her English was spot on. Her family's dream was for Gisele' to graduate from a prestigious university and become a doctor so she could return to their home in Zambia and offer help to their local communities. That dream drove them to leave everyone behind and come to America. Both of her parents had to work two and sometimes three jobs to make ends meet. Gisele', since the age of 10, was responsible for the home and caring for her three younger siblings.

Being accepted to the university was unbelievable to her. After moving into the dorms, she met all of the girls on her floor the first day. She was invited to more events and welcome programs than she had time for. Her floor RA suggested that she prioritize her involvement and really connect with other students that had the most meaning to her. The first recommendation was the Black Student Alliance. Gisele' agreed to go, hoping to meet other African immigrants.

She entered the reception and began to introduce herself to the other students and advisors that were there. The conversations focused on their experiences as African-Americans. Gisele' tried to communicate to them that she preferred to be identified as just African, but was quickly corrected that "African-American" was the better term to use. It commanded more respect for a black student than being just African. Gisele' was confused and offended. She was proud of her culture and heritage. She looked around and couldn't single out any other African students in the room. Why wouldn't they be in attendance? Surely there were other African students on campus!

Following the reception, the business meeting was called to order. Item #4 on the agenda was "End of Semester Campus-Wide Kwanzaa Celebration." The RA that invited her spoke up and suggested that Gisele' head up the committee since she knew so much about Kwanzaa. Put on the spot, Gisele' felt uncomfortable and self-conscious. She spoke up and explained that her family is Christian and celebrates Christmas, but not Kwanzaa. Kwanzaa isn't African. She'd be glad to lead the Christmas celebration committee, though. In short order, Gisele' was told that they do not celebrate Christmas on this campus, and that Kwanzaa was African.

Gisele' and her RA walked back to their dorm after the meeting. Gisele' tried to explain how important her Christian faith was to her, and she couldn't compromise it by celebrating something else. To clarify, her RA asked her if she was a "*conservative Christian, - like a republican."* Gisele' answered yes, her family held conservative views and loved that in America everyone can decide what they agree with and can vote that way.

Over the next few days, the word spread that Gisele' wasn't a "real African-American" and was a republican. A few girls asked her over lunch in the dining hall how she could believe that kind of stuff and not be loyal to blacks. Gisele' didn't see it as an "either-or." She just wanted to be true to herself and her beliefs, and be a part of the college she'd dreamed of attending for so many years. The rest of the semester in the residence hall was lonely for Gisele'. She wasn't fitting into the category that students, staff, and faculty had expected. Rather than being celebrated for her accomplishments and beliefs, she was viewed as different.

National Association of Student Personnel Administrators in Higher Education (NASPA), the national organization for student affairs professionals, defines student affairs as:

About Student Affairs

Student affairs is a critical component of the higher education experience. The work done by student affairs professionals helps students begin a lifetime journey of growth and self-exploration.

WHO WE ARE

Student learning doesn't only happen in a classroom. Opportunities for teaching and development exist everywhere on campus, and it is the responsibility of student affairs professionals to seize these moments and promote positive interactions. Encouraging an understanding of and respect for diversity, believing in the worth of individuals, and supporting students in their development are just some of the core concepts of the student affairs profession. NASPA understands the importance of student affairs work and provides opportunities for our members to continue to expand their knowledge and skills.

Student affairs departments and offices are no safe haven for conservative students. It begins the day of move-in. Parents excitedly drop off their children, help move them by carrying in boxes, sweating in lines to pick up their ID cards, and check into their residence hall. And then the tears flow, children stand on the steps of their dorm waving goodbye to their parents. And it begins. The honeymoon is already over, at least for conservative students.

If incoming students haven't already completed their online orientation, they are required to attend a campus-wide orientation. All the rules are laid out under a pretty candy coating, campus culture being the focus of the orientation. Some great things are covered that students do need to know: where resource offices are, how the health center works, how to purchase books at the bookstore. They're told how to report if they've been subjected to protected class discrimination, harassment, sexual assault or other forms of sexual misconduct, intimate partner violence or stalking. They are introduced to the office of victims assistance and the counseling center, as well as campus police. All of these orientation modules are intended to keep students safe and to know how to get help when they need it. There's also an orientation on how to be inclusive and respectful, and are warned and instructed that the campus is inclusive to everyone, and proudly so! All campus students, staff, and faculty are expected to be supportive, warmhearted, and welcoming.

They then return to their residence hall and have a housing orientation. They will have their first mandatory floor meetings at which all students are required to state their preferred pronouns. This meeting also covers topics such as bystander training. This training covers the policies that the Office of Institutional Equity and Compliance (OIEC) is responsible for to ensure that the campus community is aware of prohibited conduct, options for reporting, the obligation to report policy-related concerns, resolution processes, what resources are available to the campus community, how to offer support, and safe and effective strategies for addressing concerns or intervening as bystanders. The floor orientation also discusses gender inclusivity, racial equity, roommate agreements, white privilege, and the restorative justice and conflict resolution process.

Another important topic that is discussed is how to request roommate changes. Students are assigned randomly. Oftentimes students are assigned with a transgender or Bi student. Although philosophically a student may not disagree with any of those lifestyles, it may be an entirely different challenge to room with these students.

Students that identify as Trans are placed with students of the same gender identity. Therefore, a biological male identifying as a female will be placed with another female. This obviously would cause some very uncomfortable situations within a small dorm room or the floor restroom. Gay or Bi students are also placed randomly.

One of the harsh realities of living in residence halls is that sexual intimacy is allowed within a dorm room. It's uncomfortable enough for a student to be in the same 12x12 room with another person of the same gender having a heterosexual experience in the next bed. It becomes far more difficult to observe a homosexual experience happening when students were not prepared for this. Room change requests are put on a list and when a room becomes available within the same price range or room type the next student on the list will be notified. If a student insists on an immediate room change, they are labeled as homophobic or transphobic and may be referred to the counseling center.

Once the student gets to the counseling center, they're most likely referred to a student therapy group with up to 10 other students participating. Students that are seen at the counseling center in private sessions are students that are "urgent," meaning they have suicidal ideation, a drug or alcohol addiction, or a mental health diagnosis. All other students are referred to a peer therapy group. This poses so many problems for our conservative students.

Whether they're going to the counseling center because they feel that they're experiencing difficulty with the sexuality of their roommate, bias in the dorms, in the classroom, with roommates, or with any student affairs staff, they are certainly not going to go to a counseling center group and "out" themselves in front of other students. Few students would have the courage to do that.

The irony and hypocrisy is that bias is not tolerated on campus. There are numerous avenues to report any number of bias motivated actions or behaviors, with the exception of bias against conservatives. Bias against conservatives is tolerated.

Imagine you're a student sitting in the dining hall having lunch with the other students on your floor. You've just met them and this is a nice casual lunch to get to know the kids on your floor. The other students start making fun of conservatives, making fun of kids that are Christians and that hold conservative Christian beliefs and values. They are making fun of kids that have a more difficult time accepting various kinds of sexual expression. Where is that student supposed to go to get help? In all of their orientation sessions, nothing has been mentioned about support services for conservative students.

There's no place on campus for this student to go. If they have not already created a support system prior to entering campus, or prior to the semester if they are a transfer or a returning student, they're alone, they're distressed, and they're afraid to talk. There's no office to report this to. The OIEC office will support any student that says 'a boy stares at me and it makes me uncomfortable,' or similar complaints. If someone is made to feel uncomfortable, the offending student will be called into the OIEC office and there will be an investigation against him or her and charges may be filed for harassment.

However, in housing, a student will have to endure being in the same small dorm room with their roommate in the bed next to them having sex - heterosexual or homosexual - it doesn't matter. The staff will not support the student that's offended by being subject to their roommate's sexual behavior. Behind the scenes, staff has chuckled at the conservative student that has issues with this. They say things like, "They will grow up here!" The question in my mind was always, "What grown ups commonly and nonchalantly have sex in front of each other?" It's not within our typical social mores. But, that's what happens to students on campus.

Student affairs does not support conservative students; they support students of color, students of various sexual identities, first generation students (students that are the first in their family to attend college), and "marginalized" students of all kinds. The student affairs professionals will tell you that they advocate for all the students. Student affairs professionals will tell you that they are there for everybody. Student affairs professionals will paint the most beautiful picture of the experience your student will have on campus. Once your student gets there and is not having that experience, it's likely your fault or your student's fault. It will not be their fault for providing disparate support and advocacy for your student compared to their liberal peers.

Student affairs is as biased as academic affairs and the institution in general. This insight empowers parents to create a strategy for their students. Student affairs professionals will assure you that this is not necessary; however, it's highly necessary. As research shows, students that don't feel heard, students that feel compromised, don't thrive and may suffer from anxiety and depression and oftentimes contemplate leaving the institution altogether.

The liberal bias affects the conservative student affairs staff as well. My story in chapter one illustrated the personal and professional withdrawal and sequestration that occurred over time as a result of having no trust in the colleagues surrounding me.

A recent study reveals the experience of conservative student affairs staff. The study highlights the lose-lose position of student affairs professionals. If they speak out and advocate for themselves and other conservatives on campus, especially their conservative students, they are compromised socially and professionally. If they remain silent, they bear the emotional burden of knowing they are retreating from their truth and from justice for their students.

[39]*Public universities are often perceived as predominantly liberal environments where conservative voices are silenced. This stands in contrast to the idea that higher education, and student affairs in particular, should foster an environment in which multiple perspectives are valued. In this narrative study, we share the stories of ten self-identified conservative student affairs professionals and their experience at a public institution of higher education. To inform our study, we used the spiral of silence theory, which suggests individuals having opinions diverging from the majority will remain silent about their beliefs rather than face negative consequences. Data analysis and findings provide an understanding of how conservative ideology influenced relationships, professional engagement and overall work environment.*

Supporting different perspectives is purportedly a cornerstone of student affairs values (ACPA & NASPA, 2015; Evans & Reason, 2001). Conversely, our participants described a work environment where they choose to disengage and retreat to silence because of perceived negative consequences. The findings suggest our participants perceived a double standard in student affairs, especially regarding inclusivity of sociopolitical identity. These narratives are concerning if our participants feel they cannot disagree with their colleagues or share divergent opinions. When values of a profession are applied inconsistently to different viewpoints, there is risk of compromising the integrity of those values.

39 www.RISEstudentcoaching.com/resources

Sasha had changed dramatically in her first three years at an elite Christian college. She left home a strong, intelligent, outspoken young woman craving to learn and grow, and intent on changing the world. At home in her small rural community, she was a very left-leaning liberal. Embracing everyone's individual journey, Sasha believed she was going to be the most liberal student on campus. Coming from a small town in the northwest she felt she was a very open-minded liberal and loving. She was looking forward to her college experience and believed that she would be there to support anyone that needed any extra help because of her strong Christian beliefs.

Once on campus, she discovered an entirely different reality. Her small Christian College was as liberal as the other campuses that she and her parents had visited and toured. She moved through her first year in shock, but still adapting to campus life and the rigors of academia. Sasha, being a confident, well-spoken young woman, attempted to speak with her student affairs staff: her RAs and her Hall Directors. She quickly learned that they would not support her. Their goal was for her to adapt to the institution, not for the institution to support her.

Her parents struggled to understand what was happening. Their impression of the college was formed from their initial campus tour, move-in week, and the times that they went for parents weekend. Sasha's parents realized that they mow the grass, they clean up the flower beds and they make everything look as welcoming as possible for the parents, but the parents don't see behind the curtain, and what they're doing to their child to force conformity and compliance.

Throughout Sasha's second and third years, she became increasingly depressed. Undoubtedly her ideal campus was not ideal and did not support her fundamental Christian beliefs. By her fourth year, she was so disheartened by the classes, the faculty, and the administration's policies that she wanted to transfer to another school where she might thrive and be able to participate in classes, but was unable to because her goal was to enter a graduate program. Transferring at that point would have been academically detrimental to her graduate application. She chose to stay. A girl who was once bubbly, excited, vivacious, a leader, a liberal loving open-minded young woman became withdrawn, dark and depressed.

I have heard conservative students mocked by student affairs staff. "They have so far to go. I get where they grew up, but they're just not going to make it in this world." "Can you believe they think that's such a big deal?" and maybe the worst that I ever heard was a Hall Director saying, "I wish they would just leave. He's always complaining and his parents keep calling every week. They call and I tell them the same thing: there's nothing I can do, the student just needs to adjust to his roommate's lifestyle. I wish we could just move him to a different Hall and get him out of my way." That student needed someone that would listen and someone that would advocate for him. But that's not what he got from the touchy-feely student affairs staff. He had to adapt to the campus norm of progressive acceptance of most any behavior in a dorm room.

Counseling and therapy is not necessarily the answer because the student isn't wrong or flawed. There's nothing wrong with conservative students' sense of morals and values. It's not wrong for them to desire and expect safety and security in their living space. It's the system that is biased against them that's wrong.

They need a personal coach, someone that's outside the system that can advise them and, when necessary, advocate for them and their parents. They need to learn the skills to navigate these unwelcoming waters. Parents need to know what questions to ask before their student enrolls and before they put their money down. Once a student is there, parents need to be able to ask the right questions, ask for the right people to talk to, and to know where to go for help.

The RISE Student Coaching program is ideal. It supports the student's beliefs and values. Their coach treats the student with respect and honor and dignity. A RISE coach's goal is to build their life skills, and their resilience to be successful in their degree program and in pursuing their professional dreams.

CHAPTER 4

The Student

STUDENT DEVELOPMENT

What was once considered a simple linear trajectory of development for adolescents no longer applies. Centuries ago, development was considered completely biological. As science and research evolved, the ability to look at more complex factors has appeared. A 1904 book by G. Stanley Hall, *Adolescence*, characterized adolescence as a time of psychological and biological turmoil. That had been followed up by several other studies throughout the century. Research is now looking at adolescence and early adulthood through a new lens. This lens reflects the complexity of the world that young adults are now living in. They take into account factors such as biological development, but also parenting, how community impacts the child, and social institutions. [40]Katie Silver writing for the BBC News reports, "Adolescence now lasts from the ages of 10 to 24, although it used to be thought to end at 19."

---

40 www.RISEstudentcoaching.com/resources

In the past, researchers tended to conduct research designed to examine the impact of hormones on adolescent behavior. While this work continues, there is now an appreciation for the complex reciprocal relationship and interaction between biological and social environments, and the interaction between these environments and adolescent behavior (Graber, 1997).

Completion of formal education, financial independence from parents, marriage, and parenthood have all been markers of the end of adolescence and beginning of adulthood, and all of these transitions happen, on average, later now than in the past. In fact, the prolonging of adolescence has prompted the introduction of a new developmental period called *emerging adulthood* that captures these developmental changes out of adolescence and into adulthood, occurring from approximately ages 18 to 29 (Arnett, 2000).

Jean M. Twenge, Ph.D. is an American psychologist researching generational differences, including work values, life goals, and speed of development. In a recent book published by Twenge, *"IGen:, Why Today's Super-Connected Kids are Growing up Less Rebellious, More Tolerant, Less Happy--and Completely Unprepared for Adulthood--and What That Means for the Rest of Us,"* Twenge writes, "youths of every racial group, religion, and class are growing up more slowly." She suggests that the reason is because the world is more complicated now compared to previous generations. Our youth are bombarded with outside ideas, expectations, and the belief they have less control over their lives. Today's college students are tied in knots trying to reconcile their students' increasing care for others with the importance of having open dialogue about difficult subjects.

"Disinvitations to campus speakers are at an all-time high, more students believe the first amendment is outdated, and some faculty have been fired for discussing race in their classrooms. Comedians are steering clear of college campuses because they're afraid to offend."

"Crowds" are an emerging level of peer relationships in adolescence. In contrast to friendships and cliques, crowds are characterized more by shared reputations or images than actual interactions (Brown & Larson, 2009). These crowds reflect different prototypic identities (such as jocks or brains) and are often linked with adolescents' social status and peers' perceptions of their values or behaviors.

Living in an increasingly complex world, children are finding it increasingly complex to mature into adulthood.

STUDENT DEVELOPMENT THEORIES

One professor questioned how conservative students can develop a sense of integrity and who they are in the world in an environment that won't allow them to speak freely or think critically. To address this question, a basic understanding of child and student development theories is necessary.

What is student development theory?

Student development is the way that a student grows, progresses, or increases his or her developmental capacities as a result of enrollment in an institution of higher education. Colleges and universities rely heavily on a number of student development theories.

There are three types of development:

1. *Change* is an altered state, which may be positive or negative and progressive or regressive.
2. *Growth* is an expansion, but may be positive or negative to overall functioning.
3. *Development* is positive growth.

These definitions are critical to understand as students move through the stages of development in an environment that is hostile or unsupportive; one can see that they can easily move forward or backward in their development. This is what parents and students need to know in order to prepare themselves and to find ways to move forward regardless of the environment. These three types of development are an integral component of the developmental assessment process.

There are five main student developmental theoretical categories. Each theory details how college administrative professionals can analyze and understand college students' behavior, growth, and development.

The student developmental theoretical categories are:

1. *Psychosocial*:

College administrative professionals can use Erik Erikson's psychosocial theory to examine the various identity crises that college students may experience, such as identity versus role confusion. By understanding these challenges, professionals can provide appropriate support and guidance to help students navigate their self-identity and establish a sense of purpose.

2. *Cognitive-Structural*:

Within Jean Piaget's cognitive-structural theory, college administrative professionals can analyze how students' thinking patterns and intellectual abilities evolve throughout their college years. They can assess students' ability to solve complex problems, think critically, and engage in abstract reasoning, adapting their educational strategies accordingly.

3. *Person-Environment*:

Using the person-environment theory, college administrative professionals can assess the interaction between college students and their environment. They can examine factors such as physical spaces, social networks, and cultural influences to understand how these aspects impact students' development. This knowledge can guide professionals in creating a supportive and inviting campus environment.

4. *Humanistic-Existential*:

College administrative professionals can apply humanistic-existential theories, such as those of Carl Rogers and Abraham Maslow, to understand students' self-actualization and personal growth. By fostering an environment that values individual autonomy, self-reflection, and personal fulfillment, professionals can encourage students to explore their passions, goals, and values.

5. *Moral Development*:

College administrative professionals can utilize Lawrence Kohlberg's theory of moral development to analyze students' ethical reasoning and decision-making processes. By understanding the stages of moral development, professionals can promote moral awareness and guide students in developing a strong ethical framework that influences their behavior and choices.

By employing these theoretical categories, college administrative professionals can gain valuable insights into college students' behavior, growth, and development, allowing them to provide targeted support and enhance the overall college experience.

Each theory is used by higher education professionals in order to help students transition into collegiate life. Understanding these theories will show that the college administrators that have taken on the responsibility to facilitate students growth and development (as well as taking huge tuition dollars) are defrauding parents and students only to further their progressive agenda. It is impossible to facilitate student developmental models *and* press conservative students into "woke" cultures and experiences with positive expectant outcomes. The results are incongruous. Professionals that espouse that it is possible to achieve both simultaneously are either being deceptive or do not understand student development.

The following are some of the accepted theories used by colleges and universities.

<u>Maslow's Hierarchy of Needs</u>

This theory is foundational to student development theories. It is the most simple and significant way to look at human development. Maslow's Hierarchy is foundational to the premise of this book. Until one is assured that their physiological needs are met, and they experience safety and security, they are unable to fully pass through the next stages of development.

Students experience insecurity in campus housing when they are left to feel "less than" or like "the other." This happens in social circles as well as in their dorm hall and room. Their dorm room, or apartment if that's the case, should be their sanctuary and safe place for respite. Too often it is perceived by students as threatening or hostile. If conversations in the dining hall become too contemptuous, their basic needs will be neglected.

Without the ability for conservative students to move along the hierarchy of needs, they become stuck and aren't able to achieve the higher levels that one would hope for during this time of life. Student development is the responsibility of campus; to provide a supportive environment in which to learn and grow. Woke campuses, instead, prohibit growth by denying students a safe space to discover and evolve as people.

Psychosocial Theories

Psychosocial Theories deal with interpersonal and identity development of students: including how students define themselves, their relationships with others, and what they want to do with their lives. They examine the content of the important issues people face in their lives, such as their relationships with others and how to best shape their future.

Arthur Chickering and Linda Reisser: Theory of Identity Development

Chickering used 7 vectors to describe his theory of development:

VECTOR 1: Developing Competence: Intellectual, physical and interpersonal, physical and manual skills.

Developing competence involves acquiring and honing various skills in different domains. Here are examples of developing competence in intellectual, physical, interpersonal, and manual skills:

1. Intellectual Competence:
   - Learning a new language: Taking classes, practicing vocabulary and grammar, and engaging in conversations to develop fluency.
   - Acquiring programming skills: Studying programming languages, solving coding challenges, and building projects to enhance coding proficiency.
   - Developing critical thinking: Engaging in debates, analyzing complex problems, and evaluating different perspectives to improve analytical skills.
2. Physical Competence:
   - Mastering a sport: Practicing regularly, receiving coaching, and participating in competitions to enhance skills such as agility, coordination, and endurance.
   - Learning to play a musical instrument: Attending lessons, practicing regularly, and performing in front of an audience to improve dexterity and musicality.

- Training in martial arts: Practicing various techniques, sparring with partners, and progressing through belt levels to develop strength, flexibility, and self-defense skills.

3. Interpersonal Competence:

- Effective communication: Participating in public speaking courses, engaging in group discussions, and actively listening to others to improve clarity, empathy, and persuasion skills.
- Conflict resolution: Learning negotiation strategies, practicing empathy, and seeking win-win solutions to resolve conflicts and maintain healthy relationships.
- Leadership development: Taking on leadership roles, organizing team projects, and providing guidance and inspiration to develop leadership qualities.

4. Manual Competence:

- Woodworking: Learning to use different tools, understanding woodworking techniques, and building projects such as furniture or sculptures to develop craftsmanship skills.
- Cooking and culinary skills: Learning various cooking techniques, experimenting with recipes, and mastering different cuisines to become proficient in the kitchen.
- Automotive repair: Acquiring knowledge of vehicle systems, practicing maintenance tasks, and troubleshooting and fixing common car problems to develop mechanical skills.

VECTOR 2: Managing Emotions: Ability to recognize and accept emotions and appropriately express and control them.

Here are some examples of managing emotions:

1. Recognizing emotions:
   - Identifying when you feel angry, sad, happy, or anxious.
   - Acknowledging and understanding the intensity of your emotions.
   - Being aware of how your emotions influence your thoughts and behaviors.
2. Accepting emotions:
   - Acknowledging that it is normal to experience a wide range of emotions.
   - Allowing yourself to feel and accept your emotions without judgment.
   - Understanding that emotions provide valuable information about your needs and desires.
3. Expressing emotions appropriately:
   - Communicating your feelings clearly and respectfully to others.
   - Expressing your emotions in a way that aligns with the situation and the people involved.
   - Using effective communication skills such as active listening and nonviolent communication.
4. Controlling emotions:
   - Regulating emotional reactions to avoid impulsive or harmful behaviors.

- Employing stress-management techniques to calm oneself during challenging situations.
- Developing coping strategies to handle intense emotions in a healthy manner.

5. Practicing emotional intelligence:
   - Empathizing with others and understanding their emotional experiences.
   - Being able to regulate and manage emotions in social interactions.
   - Using emotional intelligence to navigate conflicts and build positive relationships.
6. Cultivating resilience:
   - Bouncing back from setbacks or failures by managing and processing emotions effectively.
   - Maintaining a positive outlook and finding ways to adapt in the face of adversity.
   - Seeking support from others when needed to help manage and cope with challenging emotions.

Overall, managing emotions involves self-awareness, acceptance, effective expression, and control, leading to healthier emotional well-being and improved relationships with oneself and others.

VECTOR 3: Moving Through Autonomy Toward Interdependence: Increase emotional freedom and independence, self-direction, problem solving, and awareness of interconnectedness with others.

1. Emotional Freedom:

   An example of moving through autonomy toward interdependence in terms of emotional freedom could be an individual who has developed a strong sense of self-awareness and emotional intelligence. They have learned to recognize and understand their own emotions, allowing them to express themselves authentically and without fear of judgment. This emotional freedom enables them to form deeper and more meaningful connections with others, as they can communicate their needs and emotions effectively.

2. Self-Direction:

   Moving towards interdependence involves developing self-direction while recognizing the importance of collaboration and support from others. For instance, imagine a student who takes the initiative to set personal goals, create a study plan, and manage their time effectively. They seek guidance and resources when needed but are confident in their ability to make decisions and take responsibility for their own learning. By balancing self-direction with openness to input from others, they foster a sense of interdependence and create a collaborative learning environment.

3. Problem Solving:

   Increasing interdependence involves honing problem-solving skills while valuing collective efforts. For example, within a team project at work, an individual actively contributes their unique perspective and expertise to identify and analyze problems. They encourage collaboration, facilitate brainstorming sessions, and ensure that all team members have an equal opportunity to contribute their ideas. By recognizing the interconnectedness of team members' strengths and leveraging diverse viewpoints, they enhance problem-solving capabilities and foster a sense of collective ownership.

4. Awareness of Interconnectedness:

   Developing awareness of interconnectedness involves recognizing and appreciating the impact of one's actions on others and the larger system. For instance, consider an environmentally conscious individual who actively engages in sustainable practices. They reduce their carbon footprint, recycle, and make informed choices about consumption. Furthermore, they educate others about the importance of environmental conservation and inspire them to adopt similar behaviors. By embracing their interconnectedness with the environment and society, they promote a sense of interdependence and work towards collective well-being.

5. Interpersonal Relationships:

   Moving through autonomy toward interdependence also entails nurturing healthy and balanced interpersonal relationships. For example, imagine an individual who values their independence but also recognizes the significance of meaningful connections. They actively work on building and maintaining relationships based on mutual trust, respect, and open communication. They understand that interdependence in relationships requires both giving and receiving support, fostering a sense of shared responsibility and emotional connection.

These examples illustrate how individuals can move through autonomy toward interdependence by increasing emotional freedom, self-direction, problem-solving abilities, and an awareness of interconnectedness with others.

VECTOR 4: Developing Mature Interpersonal Relationships: Develop intercultural and interpersonal tolerance, appreciate differences; create healthy, lasting, intimate relationships and friendships.

Here are some examples to illustrate these concepts:

1. Intercultural Tolerance:
    - Engaging in cultural exchange programs to understand and appreciate different cultures.
    - Participating in intercultural events and festivals to celebrate diversity.
    - Learning about different traditions, customs, and practices without judgment.
    - Seeking out friendships with people from different cultural backgrounds.
    - Actively listening and empathizing with others' experiences and perspectives.
2. Interpersonal Tolerance:
    - Respecting and accepting individual differences, including different personalities, beliefs, and values.
    - Practicing active listening to understand others' viewpoints without interrupting or dismissing them.
    - Avoiding prejudice or stereotypes and treating each person as an individual.
    - Embracing constructive feedback and being open to self-improvement.

- Demonstrating patience and understanding during conflicts or disagreements.

3. Appreciating Differences:

   - Acknowledging and valuing the unique qualities and strengths that individuals bring to a relationship.
   - Celebrating diversity and embracing different perspectives as opportunities for personal growth.
   - Seeking out diverse social circles and intentionally interacting with people from various backgrounds.
   - Challenging personal biases and prejudices through self-reflection and education.
   - Engaging in discussions that promote understanding and bridge cultural or interpersonal gaps.

4. Healthy, Lasting Intimate Relationships and Friendships:

   - Building trust and fostering open communication with one's partner or friends.
   - Respecting boundaries and supporting personal growth and autonomy.
   - Practicing empathy and compassion towards the emotions and needs of others.
   - Cultivating shared interests and activities that strengthen the bond.
   - Nurturing a sense of commitment and investing time and effort into maintaining the relationship.

Remember, these examples provide a general understanding of the concepts, but developing mature interpersonal relationships is an ongoing process that requires continuous effort, self-reflection, and open-mindedness.

> *VECTOR 5: Establishing Identity:* Acknowledge differences in identity development based on gender, ethnic background, and sexual orientation. Comfort with body and appearance, self-acceptance and self-esteem.

Here are some examples of the "establishing identity" process:

1. Gender Identity Development:

    - Boys and girls may have different experiences when it comes to establishing their gender identity. Boys might be encouraged to conform to traditional masculine norms, such as being strong and assertive, while girls might be socialized to be nurturing and conform to feminine ideals.

2. Ethnic Identity Development:

    - Individuals from different ethnic backgrounds may have diverse experiences and processes of developing their ethnic identity. For example, members of ethnic minority groups might navigate issues of assimilation, acculturation, and maintaining cultural heritage.

    - People from immigrant families may face the challenge of balancing their original cultural identity with the pressures of adapting to a new culture. This process can involve exploring and embracing their ethnic heritage while integrating into the broader society.

3. Comfort with Body and Appearance:

    - Body image development can be influenced by various factors, such as cultural beauty standards, media portrayals, and peer comparisons. Different genders and ethnic backgrounds might experience unique challenges and pressures related to body ideals.
    - Body positivity movements have emerged to promote self-acceptance and challenge narrow beauty standards. Individuals may engage in activities that boost their comfort with their bodies and foster a healthy relationship with their appearance.

4. Self-Acceptance and Self-Esteem:

    - Establishing self-acceptance and self-esteem can be influenced by personal, social, and cultural factors. For example, cultural values, family expectations, and societal messages may impact how individuals perceive themselves.
    - Differences may exist in the processes of self-acceptance and self-esteem based on gender and ethnic backgrounds. Some individuals may face particular barriers, such as gender stereotypes or racial discrimination, that can affect their self-worth.
    - Building self-acceptance and self-esteem often involves a journey of self-reflection, self-care, and cultivating a positive mindset. It can be supported through various practices, such as therapy, mindfulness, and positive affirmations.

It's important to note that these examples are generalizations, and individual experiences may vary widely within each group.

Understanding and acknowledging these differences can help create a more inclusive and supportive environment for identity development.

> *VECTOR 6: Developing Purpose:* Develop career goals, make commitments to personal interests and activities, establish strong interpersonal commitments and intentionality.

Here are examples of college students developing purpose in different areas:

1. Developing Career Goals:
    - Setting a goal to graduate with a degree in computer science and pursue a career as a software engineer at a leading technology company.
    - Participating in internships or co-op programs to gain industry experience and refine career goals in fields like marketing, finance, or healthcare.
    - Engaging in informational interviews with professionals in their desired field to gain insights and make informed decisions about their career path.
2. Making Commitments to Personal Interests and Activities:
    - Joining a student organization related to their passion for environmental sustainability and committing to organizing awareness campaigns and eco-friendly initiatives on campus.
    - Participating in community service projects, such as tutoring underprivileged children or volunteering at a local shelter, to give back and make a positive impact on others.

- Taking up a leadership role in a sports club, dance team, or theater group to develop skills, pursue personal interests, and build a strong network of like-minded individuals.

3. Establishing Strong Interpersonal Commitments:

    - Taking the initiative to form study groups with classmates to foster collaboration, exchange knowledge, and support each other's academic goals.
    - Joining a peer mentoring program to provide guidance and support to younger students, helping them navigate college life and academic challenges.
    - Participating actively in campus clubs or organizations by attending meetings, organizing events, and forming meaningful connections with fellow students.

4. Demonstrating Intentionality in Relationships:

    - Actively seeking out networking opportunities, such as attending career fairs or industry conferences, to connect with professionals and build relationships for future career prospects.
    - Cultivating meaningful relationships with professors or academic advisors by seeking their guidance, attending office hours, and actively participating in class discussions.
    - Building a supportive social circle by engaging in meaningful conversations, attending campus events, and being open to forming diverse friendships.

These examples showcase how college students can develop purpose by focusing on their career goals, personal interests, interpersonal commitments, and intentionality. By actively engaging in these areas, students can enhance their college experience, explore their passions, and lay the foundation for a successful future.

> *VECTOR 7: Developing Integrity:* Humanizing values and personalizing values and developing congruence.

Developing integrity is an important aspect of personal and ethical growth for college students. Here are some examples of how college students can demonstrate integrity:

1. Humanizing Values:

    - Volunteering: College students can humanize values by engaging in volunteer work that aligns with their personal values. For example, they can dedicate their time to helping local communities, advocating for social justice, or supporting environmental causes.

    - Participating in Service-Learning: By participating in service-learning programs, students can integrate their academic studies with community service. This approach allows them to humanize their values by applying their knowledge to real-world situations and positively impacting others.

    - Engaging in Dialogue and Empathy: College students can develop integrity by engaging in open and respectful dialogue with peers and individuals from diverse backgrounds. This includes actively listening to others' perspectives, empathizing with their experiences, and developing a greater understanding of different values and viewpoints.

2. Personalizing Values:

- Ethical Decision-Making: College students can demonstrate integrity by personalizing their values when faced with ethical dilemmas. They can critically assess the consequences of their choices, consider their personal values, and make decisions that align with their individual sense of integrity.
- Reflective Writing and Journaling: By engaging in reflective writing and journaling, students can explore their personal values, beliefs, and experiences. This practice allows them to deepen their understanding of themselves and develop a greater sense of congruence between their values and actions.
- Seeking Mentorship and Guidance: College students can seek mentorship from individuals who embody values they admire and wish to develop within themselves. By learning from mentors' experiences and wisdom, students can personalize their values and strengthen their commitment to integrity.

3. Developing Congruence:

- Academic Integrity: Upholding academic integrity is an essential aspect of developing congruence for college students. This involves avoiding plagiarism, maintaining honesty in assignments and exams, and giving proper credit to sources.
- Consistency in Actions: Students can develop congruence by aligning their actions with their values consistently. This means demonstrating integrity not only in academic settings

but also in personal relationships, extracurricular activities, and other aspects of their lives.

- Reflecting on Mistakes and Learning from Them: Developing congruence requires acknowledging and reflecting on mistakes. College students can learn from their missteps, take responsibility for their actions, and make changes to ensure their behavior aligns with their values in the future.

By humanizing values, personalizing values, and developing congruence, college students can cultivate integrity and lead lives that are grounded in ethical principles.

Scholossberg's Transition Theory

4 Major factors that influence a person's ability to cope in transition

Situation - Trigger and timing of situation, persons control, if situation causes a role change, duration, previous experience with transitions, concurrent stress, and assessment of transition.

Example of Situation:

Sarah is a college student in her junior year. The trigger for her situation is receiving an acceptance letter to study abroad for a semester in France. The timing of the situation is right before the start of the next semester.

Control:

Sarah has control over whether she chooses to accept the opportunity to study abroad or not. She can decide whether she wants to embark on this new experience or continue her regular studies on campus.

Role Change:

If Sarah decides to study abroad, the situation will cause a role change for her. She will transition from being a regular on-campus student to an international student studying in France. She will have to adapt to a new academic environment, cultural norms, and living arrangements.

Duration:

The duration of this transition will be one semester, which is typically around four to six months. Sarah will have to adjust to her new surroundings and make the most of her time studying abroad before returning to her home university.

Previous Experience with Transitions:

Sarah has not previously experienced such a significant transition. She has lived and studied in her hometown throughout her college years. This will be her first time living independently in a foreign country and adapting to a different academic system.

Stress:

Along with the excitement of studying abroad, Sarah may experience extra stress due to the new challenges she will face. She may worry about language barriers, homesickness, making new friends, and managing academic expectations in a foreign environment. The pressure to succeed academically while navigating cultural differences can also contribute to her stress.

Assessment of Transition:

Sarah's transition to studying abroad can be assessed based on her ability to adapt to the new environment, build a support network, and manage the academic workload. Her personal growth, cultural competence, and overall experience will also be important factors in assessing the success of her transition. It is crucial to provide support and resources to help her navigate any challenges she may encounter during this time. Regular check-ins with advisors and mentors can be helpful in monitoring her progress and ensuring a smooth transition.

Self - personal and demographic characters: affecting how an individual views life. Psychological Resources: aids in coping with transition.

Here's an example of a college student, highlighting their self-personal and demographic characteristics and their psychological resources that aid in coping with the transition:

Name: Emma

Self-Personal and Demographic Characteristics:

- Age: 19
- Gender: Female
- Ethnicity: Asian-American
- First-generation college student
- Introverted personality
- Raised in a small town

Psychological Resources:

- Strong sense of self-identity: Emma is proud of her cultural heritage and values her Asian-American background. This self-identity gives her a sense of belonging and helps her navigate the diverse college environment.

- Resilience: Growing up in a small town as a first-generation college student, Emma has developed resilience in the face of challenges. She believes in her ability to overcome obstacles and adapt to new situations.
- Supportive family: Emma's family has been supportive of her decision to pursue higher education. They provide emotional support and encouragement, which boosts her confidence and helps her cope with the transition to college life.
- Positive mindset: Emma has a positive outlook on life and embraces new experiences. She believes that college is an opportunity for personal growth and learning, which helps her approach challenges with optimism and open-mindedness.
- Time management skills: Emma has honed her time management skills throughout high school, balancing academics, extracurricular activities, and part-time work. This resource allows her to effectively manage her college workload and maintain a healthy work-life balance.
- Peer support: Emma has made friends within her college community who share similar experiences and goals. They provide a support system and understanding ear, allowing her to share her thoughts and concerns about college life.

These self-personal and demographic characteristics, along with the psychological resources, contribute to how Emma views life and help her cope with the transition to college.

> Support: Type, function and measurement of support as well as intimate relationships, family units, networks of friends, institutions and communities.

Here's an example of a college student named Hannah and explore the support types, functions, and measurements within different aspects of her life:

1. Support in Intimate Relationships:
   - Type: Emotional support
   - Function: Hannah's partner listens to her concerns, provides comfort, and offers encouragement during stressful times.
   - Measurement: The quality of communication, level of trust, and emotional satisfaction in the relationship can be assessed through self-report measures or relationship satisfaction scales.
2. Support in Family Units:
   - Type: Financial support
   - Function: Hannah's parents provide financial assistance to cover her tuition fees, textbooks, and living expenses while she attends college.
   - Measurement: The extent of financial support can be measured by tracking the monetary contributions made by Hannah's parents, which can be evaluated through bank statements or budget analysis.
3. Support in Networks of Friends:
   - Type: Social support
   - Function: Hannah's friends regularly spend time with her, offer advice on academic matters, and provide a support system outside of her family.

- Measurement: The strength of Hannah's friendships can be assessed through self-reported measures, such as social support scales, or by evaluating the frequency of social interactions and the depth of emotional connections.

4. Support in Institutions (e.g., College/University):

- Type: Academic support
- Function:Hannah receives guidance from her professors and academic advisors, attends tutoring sessions, and utilizes resources like the writing center to improve her academic performance.
- Measurement: The effectiveness of academic support can be measured by tracking Hannah's grades, evaluating her utilization of available resources, and conducting feedback surveys regarding her satisfaction with the support received.

5. Support in Communities:

- Type: Community engagement
- Function: Hannah actively participates in volunteer activities organized by her college, such as community service projects, charity events, or mentoring programs.
- Measurement: The level of community support can be measured by tracking Hannah's involvement in community engagement initiatives, the number of volunteer hours contributed, and through feedback from the community organizers.

These examples illustrate the different types of support, their functions, and potential ways to measure the support received by Hannah in various aspects of her college life. Keep in mind that each student's experiences and support systems may differ, and the measurements mentioned are just hypothetical examples.

> Strategies: Those that modify the situation, those that control the meaning of the problem, and those that aid in managing the stress in the aftermath.

Here are some examples of how Adam, a college student, can apply strategies in different situations:

1. Modifying the Situation:

    - Adam realizes that he is struggling to focus and study effectively in his noisy dormitory. To modify the situation, he decides to find a quieter environment for studying. He visits the library or finds a quiet café where he can concentrate better and be more productive.

    - Adam finds that he often feels overwhelmed when working on group projects. To modify the situation, he takes the initiative to schedule regular group meetings and assigns specific tasks to each member. This helps distribute the workload and ensures that everyone is accountable, reducing his stress levels.

2. Controlling the Meaning of the Problem:

    - Adam receives a lower grade on a test than he anticipated. Instead of viewing it as a failure, he controls the meaning of the problem by reframing it as an opportunity for improvement. He seeks feedback from his professor, identifies areas for growth, and develops a plan to study more effectively for future exams.

- Adam is struggling to balance his coursework with his part-time job. Instead of feeling overwhelmed, he controls the meaning of the problem by recognizing the value of time management and prioritization. He views his job as an opportunity to develop time management skills and financial independence, which helps him maintain a positive outlook.

3. Managing Stress in the Aftermath:

- After completing a challenging semester, Adam takes time to manage his stress. He engages in physical activities like going for a run or practicing yoga to relax his mind and body.
- Adam seeks support from his friends and family by discussing his academic challenges and seeking their advice and encouragement. He also seeks assistance from his college's counseling center, where he can talk to a professional and develop strategies to cope with stress.

These are examples. The strategies can be tailored to suit Adam's specific needs and circumstances. The key is for Adam to assess the situation, identify which strategy is appropriate, and apply it effectively to modify the situation, control the meaning of the problem, or manage stress in the aftermath.

<u>Janet Helms' STAGES OF WHITE RACIAL/ETHNIC IDENTITY DEVELOPMENT</u>

<u>Stage 1 Abandonment of Racism</u>

CONTACT – Unaware of own racial identity; does not think of oneself as "white" but as "normal." Tendency to view racism as "individual acts of meanness" rather than as an institutionalized system, and typically does not recognize or acknowledge "white privilege." Naïve curiosity or fear of people of color, usually based on stereotypes.

Example of CONTACT:

Name: Matthew

Background: Matthew is a 21-year-old college student majoring in business administration. He grew up in a predominantly white suburban neighborhood and attended a private school with a limited racial diversity. His family is financially well-off, and he has had minimal exposure to different racial backgrounds and experiences.

Beliefs and Attitudes:

1. Unaware of racial identity: Matthew does not think of himself as "white" but rather as "normal." He sees his racial identity as unremarkable and believes that race is not an important aspect of his identity.

2. View of racism: Matthew tends to view racism as individual acts of meanness or prejudice rather than as an institutionalized system. He perceives racism as isolated incidents rather than recognizing its pervasive nature in society.

3. Lack of recognition of white privilege: Matthew does not acknowledge or recognize the concept of white privilege. He believes that success or advantages in life are solely based on individual merits and hard work, disregarding the structural advantages that come with being white.

4. Naïve curiosity or fear of people of color: Due to his limited exposure to racial diversity, Matthew's interactions with people of color are often based on stereotypes. He may exhibit a

curious or fearful attitude towards individuals from different racial backgrounds.

Example Scenario:

During a sociology lecture on racial inequalities, the professor introduces the topic of white privilege. Matthew, who has little awareness of these concepts, engages in a discussion with his classmate, Lisa, who is a Latina student.

Matthew: "Hey, Lisa, I have a question. The professor was talking about white privilege today. I'm not sure I understand what that means exactly. I mean, I've never thought of myself as privileged just because of my race."

Lisa: "I can understand why it might seem confusing. White privilege doesn't mean that your life has been completely without challenges or that everything was handed to you. It's about the societal advantages and opportunities that come with being white in a system that favors whiteness."

Matthew: "But isn't it about treating everyone equally? I believe in equality and don't discriminate against anyone based on race. Isn't that enough to fight racism?"

Lisa: "Treating everyone equally is important, but it's also essential to recognize that racism goes beyond individual acts of meanness. It's a systemic issue that affects people's access to education, job opportunities, housing, and more. White privilege allows certain advantages to be more accessible to white individuals without them even realizing it."

Matthew: "I never really thought about it that way. I guess I've been ignorant about the larger system at play. It's eye-opening."

Lisa: "It's great that you're open to learning. Acknowledging the existence of white privilege and understanding its impact is an important step towards dismantling systemic racism. If you're interested, I can recommend some books and resources to help you delve deeper into these topics."

Matthew: "Yeah, I'd appreciate that. I want to educate myself and be more aware. I didn't realize how much I still have to learn. Thanks for helping me understand, Lisa."

Lisa: "No problem, Matthew. It's great to see you willing to grow. We're all on this journey together, and it's important to have these conversations. Let's keep learning and challenging ourselves."

In this scenario, Matthew initially demonstrates a lack of awareness about his racial identity, white privilege, and systemic racism. However, through his conversation with Lisa, he displays a willingness to learn and engage in self-reflection. This example highlights the potential for growth and increased awareness when individuals are open to dialogue and actively seek to challenge their preconceived notions.

DISINTEGRATION – Awareness of racism and white privilege increase as a result of personal experiences. Common emotional responses to this new information include shame, guilt, denial, anger, depression, and withdrawal. May attempt to persuade others to abandon racist thinking.

Example of DISINTEGRATION:

Liam, a college student majoring in sociology, was about to embark on a transformative journey during his sophomore year. Growing up in a predominantly white suburban neighborhood, Liam had always been shielded from the harsh realities of racism and the privileges that came with being white. However, as he delved deeper into his coursework, he began to confront the disheartening truth about systemic racism and white privilege.

It all started when Liam enrolled in a class called "Race and Ethnic Relations." The course opened his eyes to the pervasive and deeply ingrained structures that perpetuated racial inequality. As he learned about the history of racial discrimination, racial profiling, and the ongoing struggles faced by marginalized communities, Liam's worldview began to unravel.

Personal experiences further intensified Liam's awareness of racism and white privilege. He befriended individuals from diverse backgrounds, engaging in candid conversations that shed light on the daily challenges they faced due to their race. Listening to their stories of discrimination, microaggressions, and unequal opportunities, Liam felt a mix of emotions—shame, guilt, anger, and sadness.

Initially, Liam found it difficult to come to terms with the knowledge that his own privilege had contributed to the suffering of others. He experienced a deep sense of shame for having been oblivious to the extent of racial injustice. However, he recognized that acknowledging his privilege was the first step toward making a change.

As Liam grappled with this newfound awareness, he confronted his own biases and the subtle ways in which racism had influenced his thinking. He questioned his assumptions, challenging his own privilege and the privileges he witnessed in society. It was a difficult process that left him feeling overwhelmed and depressed at times.

Liam's emotional journey also involved moments of denial. He caught himself initially dismissing certain instances of racism, thinking they were isolated incidents rather than systematic problems. However, as he engaged in more conversations, conducted research, and deepened his understanding, he couldn't ignore the overwhelming evidence that racism was deeply embedded in society.

Motivated by his own experiences and growing awareness, Liam felt a strong urge to influence change. He engaged in conversations with friends, family, and classmates, attempting to persuade them to abandon racist thinking. Sometimes these discussions led to heated debates, as not everyone was receptive to his ideas. Nevertheless, Liam remained steadfast in his commitment to promoting equality and justice.

At times, the weight of his newfound awareness and the resistance he encountered caused Liam to withdraw from certain social circles. He sought solace in activist groups on campus and online communities, finding support and camaraderie among like-minded individuals who were also dedicated to dismantling racism.

Liam's journey through the disintegration phase was challenging but necessary for his personal growth and commitment to social change. Through his own experiences, education, and empathetic connections, he began to unravel the layers of racism and white privilege, gaining a deeper understanding of the injustices that persisted in society.

REINTEGRATION – May feel pressured by others to "not notice" racism. Feelings of guilt and denial are transformed into fear and anger toward people of color; a common response is to "blame the victim." Chooses to avoid the issue of racism, if possible, rather than struggling to define a non-racist identity.

Example of REINTEGRATION:

Jen, a college student, finds herself caught in the dynamics of reintegration when it comes to addressing racism. Having grown up in a predominantly white community, she has limited exposure to racial diversity and lacks awareness about systemic racism and its impact on marginalized communities.

As Jen enters college, she encounters a more diverse environment where conversations about racism are prevalent. However, instead of actively engaging with these discussions, Jen feels pressured by her peers to "not notice" racism. She experiences conflicting emotions, including guilt and denial, as she grapples with her own racial biases and the realization that racism exists.

Jen's feelings of guilt and denial gradually transform into fear and anger, often directed towards people of color. She may struggle with understanding her own privilege and may unintentionally perpetuate harmful stereotypes or engage in discriminatory behaviors. To cope with these uncomfortable emotions, she may resort to blaming the victim, rationalizing systemic inequalities, or avoiding the topic of racism altogether.

Rather than confronting the issue head-on and working towards developing a non-racist identity, Jen chooses to avoid the subject of racism whenever possible. She may steer clear of conversations or situations that force her to confront her biases, preferring to remain in her comfort zone and maintain the status quo.

Jen's journey illustrates the challenges faced by individuals in the reintegration stage, where the pressure to conform and the fear of confronting one's own complicity can hinder personal growth and contribute to the perpetuation of racism. It highlights the importance of education, self-reflection, and actively challenging one's own biases to move towards a more inclusive and anti-racist mindset.

Stage 2 Defining a Non-Racist White Identity

PSEUDO-INDEPENDENCE – Individual is abandoning beliefs in white superiority. Has an intellectual understanding of the unfairness of white privilege and recognizes personal responsibility for dismantling racism. May choose to distance oneself from other whites, and actively seek out people of color to help him/her better understand racism.

Example of PSEUDO-INDEPENDENCE:

Emma, a college student majoring in sociology, had always been aware of the concept of white privilege, but it wasn't until she took a course on race and inequality that she truly began to understand its impact. Through the course readings, discussions, and interactions with her classmates, Emma started questioning her own beliefs about race and white superiority.

As she delved deeper into the subject, Emma realized that she had a responsibility to actively dismantle racism and contribute to creating a more equitable society. She recognized that merely acknowledging her privilege was not enough; she needed to take action. Emma started educating herself on the experiences and perspectives of people of color by reading books, attending workshops, and engaging in meaningful conversations with individuals from different racial backgrounds.

In her quest for knowledge, Emma sought out friendships and mentorships with people of color. She understood that building relationships with individuals who had firsthand experiences of racism would help her gain a deeper understanding of its systemic nature. Emma listened attentively to their stories, empathized with their struggles, and learned how to be a supportive ally in the fight against racism.

While she was passionate about her newfound awareness, Emma also grappled with feelings of discomfort and guilt. She recognized that distancing herself from other white individuals could perpetuate a divide and hinder progress. Instead, Emma aimed to engage her white peers in conversations about racism and encourage them to critically examine their own biases and privilege.

Through her dedication and commitment, Emma strived to be a catalyst for change on her college campus. She organized workshops and events that addressed issues of race, privilege, and allyship, creating spaces for open dialogue and learning. Emma used her platform to raise awareness, challenge stereotypes, and advocate for social justice.

Emma's journey toward pseudo-independence was an ongoing process. She acknowledged that dismantling racism required continuous self-reflection, learning, and action. Emma was committed to using her privilege and knowledge to actively contribute to the larger movement for racial equality, recognizing that the responsibility fell not only on individuals of color, but also on white individuals like herself.

IMMERSION/EMERSION – Actively seeking to redefine whiteness. Asking yourself-questions such as "Who am I racially?" "What does it really mean to be white in the U.S.?" Needs support from other anti-racist whites who have asked similar questions. Focus is on developing a positive white identity not based on assumed superiority. Takes pride in active anti-racist stance.

Example of IMMERSION/EMERSION

Nicholas is a college student who actively engages in the process of immersion/emersion. He is committed to redefining whiteness and understanding his racial identity.

Recognizing the importance of support and learning from others who have undergone similar self-reflection, Nicholas seeks the company of anti-racist white individuals who have asked themselves these challenging questions. He believes that connecting with others on this journey can provide valuable insights and perspectives.

Nicholas's focus is on developing a positive white identity that isn't rooted in assumed racial superiority. He actively engages in anti-racist efforts and takes pride in his stance against racism. Through education, self-reflection, and collaboration, Nicholas aims to contribute to a more inclusive and equitable society.

AUTONOMY – Has internalized a positive white racial identity. Actively anti-racist within own sphere of influence. Development of racial identity is not static, and continues to be open to new information and ongoing self-examination. Able to work effectively in multiracial setting in "beloved community."

Example of AUTONOMY

College student Emily demonstrates a strong commitment to autonomy and the development of a positive white racial identity. She actively engages in anti-racist efforts within her own sphere of influence and continuously seeks to learn and grow. Emily understands that racial identity development is an ongoing process and remains open to new information and self-examination.

Emily also excels in working effectively within a multiracial setting, fostering a sense of unity and inclusivity. She values the concept of community where people from diverse backgrounds come together in a harmonious and respectful manner. Emily's actions and mindset reflect her dedication to promoting racial equality and creating a more inclusive society.

Cognitive - Structural

The mind's structures are viewed as arising at one time, always in the same order, regardless of cultural conditions, the age and rate the person travels through each stage varies. Each stage builds upon the one before it. Illuminates changes in the way people think and make decisions. Examines both intellectual and moral development.

Jean Piaget's cognitive development theory

Developed by Swiss psychologist Jean Piaget in the early 20th century, it proposes that children learn and develop through four distinct stages:

1. Sensorimotor
2. Preoperational
3. Concrete Operational
4. Formal Operational

<u>Sensorimotor Stage (birth to two years old)</u>:

During this period, infants gain knowledge of their environment through sensory experiences and motor activities. This includes exploration of objects with hands and mouth, learning to differentiate between visually similar objects, forming associations between physical objects and their functions, and understanding basic cause-and-effect relationships.

<u>Preoperational Stage (two to seven years old)</u>:

At this age, young children begin to gain an understanding of language and symbols while they are still quite limited in their ability to think abstractly or logically. They become more proficient at using symbolic thought and are able to think beyond immediate experiences.

Concrete Operational Stage (seven to 11 years old):

In this stage of development, children become better problem solvers as they start to understand logical operations such as conservation (the concept that an object stays the same even when it changes shape). They also begin to acquire skills such as classification and seriation (the ability to order items based on size or other properties).

Formal Operational Stage (11 years old onward):

At this point, teenagers are able to think hypothetically and can reason abstractly, allowing them to consider abstract concepts such as morality or religion. Additionally, they can draw conclusions from hypothetical situations as well as form hypotheses and test them via experimentation or research.

William Perry's Scheme of Intellectual and Ethical Development

William Perry's research found that college students journey through 4 stages (with 9 different "positions" defined) with respect to intellectual and moral development. These stages can be characterized in terms of the student's attitude towards knowledge.

Students progress through Perry's scheme hierarchically, although some students may stray from straight line development. The journey is sometimes repeated and one can be at different stages at the same time with respect to different subjects.

Each stage represents a different way of thinking.

The 4 stages are:

1. *Dualism/Received Knowledge:*

   Seeing the world as dichotomous: Situations are good or bad, there are right/wrong answers, seeking black or white facts, authorities have the correct answers. Students typically have trouble with reflection, comparison, and analysis because they are learning as a simple information exchange and nothing more.

2. *Multiplicity/Subjective Knowledge:*

   There are conflicting answers; therefore, students must trust their "inner voices," not external authority. Seeing there may be other answers, facts might not always tell the truth and authority isn't always correct. Everyone has a right to their own opinion. Students believe their peers are more legitimate sources of knowledge and multiple alternatives are now acceptable. Logic, data and evidence are viewed as less important, versus the amount of work done or time spent seen as key.

3. *Relativism/Procedural Knowledge:*

   There are disciplinary reasoning methods: Connected knowledge: empathetic vs. separated knowledge: "objective analysis." Students recognize the need to support opinions, while all opinions are no longer equally valid. Context is taken into account and analysis and synthesis now occur. The capacity for empathy is now present. Looking at each viewpoint or answer and seeing what makes the most sense or what is the right answer for them.

4. *Commitment to Relativism:*

    Integration of knowledge learned from others with personal experience and reflection. Students learn to tolerate ambiguity and to make choices in a contextual world. They develop a personal set of values and are able to make choices and commitments in the absence of complete information. Continual knowledge and learning becomes important. No one understands there are multiple answers and ways to view situations. Looking at each viewpoint and making a decision what is right for them and revisiting those commitments and making changes when necessary.

Baxter Magolda's Theory of Self-Authorship

The theory of self-authorship is based on several assumptions.

- Ways of knowing and patterns within them are socially constructed.
- Ways of knowing understood through naturalistic inquiry.
- There's a fluid use of reasoning patterns.
- Patterns are related to, but not directed by, gender.
- Student stories are context bound.
- Ways of knowing are patterns.

Phase 1: Absolute Knowing—allowing others to define who you are. "Young adults follow the plans laid out for them" while assuring themselves they created these plans themselves.

Example of Absolute Knowing:

Brooke, a college student, embodies the concept of "Absolute Knowing—allowing others to define who you are" and the tendency of young adults to follow predefined plans while convincing themselves they created those plans independently.

Throughout her life, Brooke had always relied on external sources to shape her identity and define her goals. As a child, she followed her parents' expectations of achieving high grades, participating in extracurricular activities, and pursuing a career in medicine, just like her physician father. She never questioned these expectations and considered them as her own desires and aspirations.

As Brooke transitioned into college, she continued to seek validation and guidance from her professors, peers, and societal norms. She chose her major based on what was deemed prestigious and lucrative rather than pursuing her genuine interests. She enrolled in pre-med courses, even though she felt an inner inclination towards art and creativity.

When it came to making decisions about her future, Brooke sought approval and direction from others. She attended career fairs and internships that aligned with societal expectations, rather than exploring her own passions and unique path. She convinced herself that she had independently crafted her plans, even though they were heavily influenced by external factors.

Deep down, Brooke yearned for a sense of authenticity and self-discovery. However, she struggled to break free from the comfort of external validation and societal expectations. She feared the uncertainty and judgment that might come from deviating from the predetermined path set by others.

Brooke's story exemplifies how young adults can unknowingly surrender their individuality and allow others to dictate their identity and life choices. By succumbing to the pressures of external influences, they may deny themselves the opportunity for self-exploration and personal growth. It serves as a reminder for individuals like Brooke to challenge the status quo, question societal expectations, and embrace their own unique journey of self-discovery.

Phase 2: Transitional Knowing—The plans a student has been following do not necessarily fit anymore, and new plans need to be established. Students are dissatisfied with themselves. Students need guidance to discover their life of purpose when they are at the "crossroads."

Here's an example of a college student named Hope going through a period of "Transitional Knowing":

Hope is a junior majoring in economics at a renowned university. Throughout her academic journey, she has been diligently following a predetermined plan that includes taking advanced economics courses and pursuing internships in finance. However, as she progresses further into her studies, she begins to feel a sense of dissatisfaction with herself and the path she's been following.

Hope starts questioning whether economics and finance truly align with her passions and values. She finds herself contemplating the idea of pursuing a career in social justice and advocacy, which she feels a deep connection to. Hope realizes that the plans she has been following may no longer be the right fit for her, and she finds herself standing at a crossroads, uncertain about her future.

Recognizing the signs of transitional knowing, the student development professionals at her college step in to provide guidance and support. They organize workshops, seminars, and career counseling sessions focused on exploring different career paths and discovering one's purpose. Hope actively participates in these opportunities, seeking advice from mentors and professionals who have successfully navigated similar crossroads.

Hope is also connected with alumni who are working in the social justice and advocacy fields. She attends panel discussions and networking events to gain insights into their experiences and learn about the various paths available in the realm of social justice work. This exposure helps her envision a new plan for herself, one that incorporates her passion for social justice.

With the guidance of the professionals, Hope explores volunteer opportunities and joins student organizations focused on advocacy and community outreach. She also starts taking relevant courses outside of her major, such as political science and sociology, to broaden her knowledge and skills in the field she is now passionate about.

Over time, Hope's dissatisfaction transforms into a sense of empowerment and excitement as she begins to carve out a new path aligned with her values and interests. She realizes that her true purpose lies in making a positive impact on society and working towards social justice.

Hope establishes a new plan for herself that involves pursuing graduate studies in social work and becoming an advocate for marginalized communities. She feels a renewed sense of purpose and drive, confident in her decision to forge a career path that aligns with her passions.

In this example, Hope's experience illustrates the importance of guidance and support when students find themselves at a crossroads. Through the assistance of student development professionals and various opportunities for exploration, Hope is able to discover her true calling and establish new plans that bring her fulfillment and purpose.

Phase 3: Independent Knowing—creating the ability to choose your own beliefs and stand up for them (especially when facing conflict or opposing views).

Jacqueline, a dedicated and curious student, exemplifies the concept of "Independent Knowing" by consistently demonstrating the ability to choose her own beliefs and confidently stand up for them, even in the face of conflict or opposing views.

For instance, during a classroom discussion on a controversial topic, Jacqueline actively engages with different perspectives and listens attentively to her classmates' arguments. Rather than simply conforming to popular opinion, she takes the time to critically analyze the information presented, considering its validity and aligning it with her own values and principles.

In a situation where her beliefs are challenged or met with opposition, Jacqueline remains steadfast and articulate in expressing her point of view. She understands the importance of respectful dialogue and is able to engage in thoughtful debates without resorting to personal attacks or aggression. Jacqueline supports her arguments with well-researched evidence and logical reasoning, allowing her to effectively communicate her position and defend her beliefs.

Jacqueline's commitment to independent knowing extends beyond the classroom. She actively seeks out diverse perspectives by reading books, articles, and engaging in meaningful discussions with individuals from various backgrounds. This helps her broaden her understanding of different viewpoints, enabling her to make informed decisions and develop a more comprehensive worldview.

By embodying the principles of independent knowing, Jacqueline becomes an inspiration to her peers. Her courage to think critically, form her own beliefs, and confidently advocate for them fosters an environment of intellectual growth and respectful dialogue, encouraging others to exercise their own independent thinking skills.

Phase 4: Contextual Knowing —"grounded in their self-determined belief system, in their sense of who they are, and the mutuality of their relationships."

Lamar is a college student who firmly believes in the power of education as a means of personal and societal transformation. He understands the value of knowledge in shaping his own identity and creating meaningful connections with others. Lamar's contextual knowing is grounded in his self-determined belief system, which emphasizes the importance of critical thinking, empathy, and social justice.

In his pursuit of knowledge, Lamar actively seeks out diverse perspectives and experiences that challenge his existing beliefs and broaden his understanding of the world. He engages in open discussions, attends lectures and workshops, and actively participates in extracurricular activities that promote inclusivity and dialogue.

Lamar's sense of who he is is deeply rooted in his commitment to making a positive impact on society. He sees himself as an agent of change, striving to address systemic issues and promote equality. He actively seeks opportunities to engage in community service, volunteer work, and advocacy campaigns related to education, social justice, and equal access to opportunities.

Lamar's contextual knowing extends beyond his personal growth; he recognizes the importance of mutuality in his relationships. He values the perspectives and experiences of others and seeks to create an inclusive environment where everyone's voices are heard and respected. He actively collaborates with his peers, professors, and community members to foster a sense of collective responsibility and co-create solutions to pressing issues.

Through his belief system, sense of self, and mutuality in relationships, Lamar embodies contextual knowing as a college student. He strives to combine his personal growth with a larger societal impact, making a positive difference in the lives of those around him.

Person - Environment

Person-environment theories consider how the college environment impacts a student's growth and behavior. Higher education professionals use them to plan activities and programs that foster a sense of community among students and to help students transition to college life academically and socially.

Emerging Adulthood, Arnett 2000

Emerging adulthood is a development theory for the period from the late teens through the twenties, with a focus on ages 18 to 25.

Emerging adulthood is a new developmental theory. It makes a distinction between adolescents and early adulthood. By definition, early adulthood establishes that an individual has reached adulthood but is in an early stage. Emerging adulthood is a distinction between adolescence and early adulthood that defines an additional developmental stage that has not been identified previously. The developmental theory recognizes that because marriage, parenthood and career choices are typically not engaged in until late 20s or perhaps early 30s, emerging adulthood defines a period in life that is neither adolescence or young adulthood.

Three areas are defined in Emerging Adulthood

1. Demographics

   During this age range, an individual's demographics can change considerably. Individuals may move in and move out of their parental home, or into a home of their own if they are working and employed.

2. Subjective Perceptions

   Emerging adults do not see themselves as adolescents, but many of them also do not see themselves entirely as adults.

3. Identity Exploration

   This is a period of life that offers the most opportunity for identity exploration in the areas of love, work, and worldviews.

Gender as a performance, Judith Butler

Gender performance is the idea that gender is something inscribed in daily practices, learned and performed based on cultural norms of femininity and masculinity.

The author, Judith Butler, questions the belief that certain gender behaviors are natural and some are performed. It is also theorized that identity itself is created externally, rather than emerging internally.

[41] *"Indeed, Butler goes far as to argue that gender, as an objective natural thing, does not exist: gender reality is performative which means, quite simply, that it is real only to the extent that it is performed." Gender, according to Butler, is by no means tied to material bodily facts but it is solely and completely a social construction, a fiction, one that, therefore, is open to change and constitution. "Because there is neither an 'essence' that gender expresses or externalizes nor an objective ideal to which gender aspires; because gender is not a fact, the various acts of gender creates the idea of gender, and without those acts, there would be no gender at all. Gender is, thus, a construction that regularly*

41 www.RISEstudentcoaching.com/resources

conceals its Genesis." That Genesis is not corporal but performative, so that the body becomes its gender only "through a series of Acts which are renewed, revised, and Consolidated Through Time." But illustrating the artificial, conventional, and historical nature of gender construction, Butler attempts to critique the assumptions of normative heterosexuality: those punitive rules (social, familial, and legal) that force us to conform to heterosexual standards for identity.

A Theory of Vocational Choice (Holland, 1959)

Holland's theory of vocational choice assumes that at the time of vocational choice, the person is the product of the interaction of their particular heredity with a variety of cultural and personal forces including peers, parents and significant adults and their social class, American culture, and the physical environment. Out of this experience, the person develops a hierarchy of habitual or preferred methods for dealing with environmental tasks. These include how they interact with the physical and social environments, their physical abilities and the individual's personal development.

Holland maintains that in choosing a career, people prefer jobs where they can be around others who are like them. They search for environments that will let them use their skills and abilities, and express their attitudes and values, while taking on enjoyable problems and roles behavior is determined by an interaction between personality and environment.

This theory is centered on the belief that most people fit into one of six personality types:

- Realistic
- Investigative

- Artistic
- Social
- Enterprising
- Conventional

Holland asserts that people of the same personality type working together in a job create an environment that fits and rewards their type.

Human - Existential

Moral

Factors that promote moral growth include cognitive development, stimulation, exposure to conflicting views. Relevant social experience is also important for children to interact with people who have differing points of view. This promotes a cognitive disequilibrium. The ability to consider different points of view allows the opportunity to sort out differences and similarities. Moral development includes our sense of right and wrong that is learned through experience of reinforcers and punishers, much as any behaviors or traits are learned. Our expectations and beliefs influence which behaviors are learned. Vicarious reinforcers such as observing peers, media, parents, and others influence our sense of right and wrong as well as actual behaviors.

Gilligan's Theory of Women's Moral Development

Level 1 - orientation to individual survival, individual is self-centered and preoccupied with survival, unable to distinguish amid necessity and wants.

Here's an example that focuses on Trinity, a college student who is self-centered and survival-oriented, struggling to differentiate between necessity and wants:

Trinity is a college student who has a highly individualistic mindset and is solely focused on her own survival. She believes that her success and well-being are paramount, often disregarding the needs and concerns of others around her. Trinity's primary concern is achieving high grades and securing a stable future for herself, which leads her to prioritize her own needs above everything else.

As a result of her self-centered nature, Trinity becomes preoccupied with survival in the college environment. She constantly worries about maintaining her academic performance and securing internships or job opportunities that she believes are necessary for her future success. Her tunnel vision causes her to overlook the importance of other aspects of the college experience, such as building meaningful relationships, participating in extracurricular activities, or contributing to the community.

Trinity's inability to distinguish between necessity and wants further exacerbates her self-centered behavior. She perceives every opportunity or material possession as crucial for her survival and success, often ignoring the line between what is truly necessary and what is merely a desire. For instance, she might prioritize purchasing the latest gadgets or trendy fashion items, believing that these possessions will enhance her social status and improve her chances of securing a desirable job in the future. In doing so, she neglects the financial strain it puts on her and overlooks more practical investments such as textbooks or savings for emergencies.

Trinity's orientation toward individual survival and her self-centeredness create a challenging college experience for her. Her narrow focus on personal success and inability to distinguish between needs and wants can lead to a lack of fulfillment and a strained social life. Her single-minded pursuit of survival may alienate her from potential friends and networking opportunities, hindering her personal and professional growth. Moreover, her fixation on individual success may prevent her from developing important skills like collaboration, empathy, and teamwork, which are valued in both academic and professional settings.

In this example, Trinity's self-centeredness and inability to differentiate between necessity and wants impacts her college experience. While her drive for personal success is understandable, her lack of consideration for others and her limited perspective on what truly matters in college may hinder her overall growth and limit her potential for a well-rounded and fulfilling educational journey.

First transition - from selfishness to responsibility, issues of attachment and connection to others integrates responsibility and care into a repertoire of moral decision-making patterns.

Ashley, a college student, initially exhibited selfishness in her behavior and decision-making. She focused primarily on her own desires and neglected the needs and well-being of others. For instance, she would often skip group projects or delegate all the work to her teammates while taking credit for their efforts.

However, as Ashley progressed through her college years, she encountered various experiences that led her to reflect on the importance of responsibility and the impact of her actions on others. One significant event was when she volunteered at a local homeless shelter during her summer break. Through this experience, Ashley witnessed firsthand the struggles and challenges faced by those less fortunate than her. This exposure ignited a sense of empathy and a realization that she could make a positive difference in the lives of others.

As Ashley's awareness of the issues of attachment and connection to others grew, she started actively seeking opportunities to build meaningful relationships and contribute to her community. She joined clubs and organizations that aligned with her interests and values, allowing her to connect with like-minded individuals and engage in projects that aimed to address social issues. By participating in group activities and collaborating with others, she began to appreciate the importance of teamwork and cooperation in achieving shared goals.

With time, Ashley integrated responsibility and care into her repertoire of moral decision-making patterns. She learned to consider the impact of her choices on others and evaluate the ethical implications of her actions. Instead of seeking personal gain at the expense of others, she started making decisions that took into account the well-being of those around her.

For instance, when presented with an opportunity to apply for a prestigious internship, Ashley considered how her acceptance would affect her fellow classmates. Realizing that her absence would leave her group project teammates in a difficult position, she made the responsible choice to decline the internship and support her peers. By prioritizing collective welfare over personal advancement, Ashley demonstrated the integration of responsibility and care into her decision-making process.

Overall, Ashley's journey from selfishness to responsibility showcases the transformative power of personal experiences and self-reflection. Through her newfound understanding of attachment and connection to others, she learned to navigate moral decision-making with a greater sense of responsibility and care for those around her.

Level 2 - goodness as self-sacrifice, survival becomes social acceptance, reflects conventional feminine values, may give up own judgment to achieve consensus and connection with others.

Grace is a college student who embodies the concept of self-sacrifice as a means to gain social acceptance. She often prioritizes the needs and desires of others over her own, going out of her way to help her friends and classmates. For example, if a friend asks for her assistance with a project, Grace willingly sacrifices her own free time and personal goals to ensure their success.

In her pursuit of social acceptance, Grace tends to conform to conventional feminine values. She adheres to societal expectations of what it means to be a woman, such as being nurturing, accommodating, and empathetic. She values harmony and connection with others, striving to maintain positive relationships and avoiding conflict at all costs.

Grace's desire for consensus and connection sometimes leads her to compromise her own judgment. She may suppress her own opinions and ideas to align with the majority or avoid upsetting others. Rather than asserting herself, she seeks to maintain harmony within her social circles, even if it means sacrificing her own authenticity.

Overall, Grace's actions and behavior reflect a strong inclination towards self-sacrifice, survival through social acceptance, and adherence to conventional feminine values. While these qualities can bring her a sense of belonging and validation, it is important for her to strike a balance between prioritizing others and considering her own needs and beliefs.

Second transition - from goodness to truth, questions why she puts others first at her own expense, examines needs to determine if they can be included in her responsibility, examines needs as truth not egotism.

Destiny is a college student known for her selfless nature and unwavering dedication to putting others first. She is deeply committed to the pursuit of goodness, always striving to make a positive impact on the people around her. However, Destiny finds herself constantly sacrificing her own well-being and neglecting her personal needs in the process. This raises questions about why she prioritizes others at her own expense and prompts her to examine her motivations more closely.

Destiny begins by exploring her reasons for putting others before herself. She realizes that her desire to help and support others stems from a genuine concern for their well-being. She genuinely wants to make a difference in their lives and believes that it is her responsibility to do so. However, she starts to wonder if there are healthier ways to approach this responsibility without compromising her own needs.

To gain a better understanding, Destiny embarks on a journey of self-reflection and introspection. She starts by examining her needs and desires, acknowledging that taking care of herself is just as important as helping others. Destiny recognizes that neglecting her own well-being can lead to burnout and prevent her from effectively assisting those around her in the long run.

Destiny also realizes that identifying and addressing her own needs is not an act of egotism but a crucial aspect of personal growth and self-care. By acknowledging her needs, she can develop a stronger sense of self and a healthier balance in her relationships. She understands that attending to her own well-being allows her to be more present, compassionate, and effective in her efforts to support others.

As Destiny delves deeper into this journey, she begins to establish healthy boundaries and learns to prioritize her own needs without compromising her commitment to goodness and truth. She recognizes that true selflessness doesn't mean sacrificing oneself completely, but rather finding a harmonious balance between taking care of oneself and being there for others.

In this way, Destiny transforms her understanding of responsibility. She learns to distinguish between the needs that are within her capacity to address and those that are beyond her control. She acknowledges that she cannot single-handedly solve everyone's problems but can offer support within her means.

Destiny's examination of her needs as truths, rather than acts of egotism, leads her to a more balanced and sustainable approach to helping others. She realizes that by taking care of herself, she becomes a stronger and more reliable source of support, ultimately enabling her to make a more meaningful and lasting impact on the lives of those she seeks to assist.

Level 3 - morality of nonviolence, elevated to care by a transformed understanding of self and redefinition of morality. A moral equivalence is established between self and others. Hurting anyone, including oneself, is seen as immoral. This is the most sophisticated form of reasoning.

Kayla, a college student, embarked on a transformative journey that led her to embrace nonviolence and develop an elevated sense of care through a profound understanding of self and a redefinition of morality. Her new perspective brought forth a moral equivalence between herself and others, wherein any act of causing harm, whether to others or oneself, was deemed morally unacceptable. This advanced form of reasoning represents the pinnacle of sophistication in moral understanding.

Kayla's transformation began with a deep reflection on her own values and beliefs. She questioned the prevailing norms of society, which often justified violence or harm in certain circumstances. As she delved into various philosophical and ethical perspectives, she encountered the teachings of nonviolence and the concept of interconnectedness.

Through her studies and introspection, Kayla gradually realized that she and others were fundamentally interconnected and shared a common humanity. She recognized that causing harm to anyone, including herself, was incompatible with this understanding. This realization shattered the traditional dichotomy between self and others, and she began to see all sentient beings as deserving of compassion and respect.

Kayla's journey toward a sophisticated understanding of morality involved grappling with difficult ethical dilemmas. She recognized that even actions that might appear justifiable or necessary in certain situations could perpetuate cycles of violence and suffering. She challenged herself to find alternative solutions rooted in empathy, understanding, and peaceful means of conflict resolution.

As Kayla embraced her newfound philosophy, she actively sought opportunities to promote nonviolence and empathy on her college campus and in her personal life. She engaged in peaceful dialogue, organized workshops and discussions, and advocated for nonviolent approaches to social issues. By embodying the principles she espoused, she aimed to inspire others to reconsider their own moral frameworks and embrace nonviolence as a transformative force.

Kayla's evolved understanding of morality represents the highest form of reasoning, as it transcends self-interest and recognizes the inherent worth and interconnectedness of all beings. She exemplifies a sophisticated and compassionate approach to ethics, striving to create a world where violence is seen as morally repugnant and nonviolence becomes the guiding principle for resolving conflicts and fostering harmonious relationships.

Piaget's Stages of Moral Development

Piaget was one of the first psychologists to specifically outline a theory of moral development. He found that while young children were focused on authority, with age they became increasingly autonomous and able to evaluate actions from a set of independent principles of morality. Piaget's theory of moral development describes two stages of moral development:

Heteronomous Morality

In the first stage of moral development, children follow strict rules and are completely obedient to authority. Piaget states that this occurs in younger children in part because of their cognitive development. He also noted that social relationships between adults and children also supported this stage: adults have a natural authority over children, and power and rules handed down without discussion.

Autonomous Morality.

As children begin to learn new things about the world and their interaction with other children and adults, they progress into the second stage of world development. In this stage, he states that children learn how to critically evaluate rules and apply them based upon cooperation and respect with other children. They begin to judge how wrong an action is by the intention of the perpetrator, and punishment is adjusted accordingly.

Kohlber's Stages of Moral Development

Kohlberg's theory holds that moral reasoning, which is the basis for ethical behavior, has six identifiable developmental stages. He followed the development of moral judgment beyond the ages originally studied by Piaget. Kohlberg's six stages were grouped into three levels: pre-conventional, conventional, and post-conventional.

Level 1 pre-conventional

The pre-conventional level of moral reasoning is especially common in children, although adults can also exhibit this level of reasoning. Reasoners in the pre-conventional level judge the morality of an action by its direct consequences. The pre-conventional level consists of the first and second stages of moral development, and are purely concerned with the self in an egocentric manner

1. Obedience and punishment oriented

   Example of Obedience and punishment orientation

   Natalie, a college student, exemplifies the pre-conventional level of moral reasoning through her obedience and punishment-oriented mindset. She believes that the morality of an action should be judged based on its direct consequences, particularly how it affects her own self-interest. Natalie is primarily concerned with avoiding punishment and gaining rewards for her actions. Her moral decisions are influenced by a fear of authority figures and a desire to conform to societal norms to avoid negative consequences. She tends to prioritize her own needs and desires over considering the broader impact of her actions on others or the larger society. For Natalie, the consequences of an action play a significant role in determining its moral worth, reflecting her pre-conventional level of moral reasoning.

2. Self-Interest Orientation

   Example of Self-Interest Orientation

   Jose, a college student, demonstrates the characteristics of the pre-conventional level of moral reasoning, specifically the self-interest orientation. He believes that the morality of an action should be evaluated based on the immediate consequences it brings to himself. Jose tends to prioritize his own personal gains and benefits when making moral decisions, often disregarding the potential impact on others or societal norms.

For example, if faced with a situation where he could cheat on a test without getting caught, Jose might consider it as a viable option. His primary concern would be avoiding negative consequences for himself, such as failing the test or damaging his academic record. He might justify his decision by arguing that as long as he personally benefits from cheating, it is morally acceptable.

In this way, Jose's moral reasoning remains egocentric and self-centered, focusing solely on his own self-interests rather than considering the broader ethical implications or the well-being of others. His decision-making is reflective of the pre-conventional level of moral development, where individuals primarily evaluate the morality of actions based on the direct consequences they bring to themselves.

Level 2 conventional

The conventional level of moral reasoning is typical of adolescents and adult persons who reason in a conventional way and judge the morality of actions by comparing these actions to societal views and expectations. The conventional level consists of the third and fourth stages of moral development.

1. Interpersonal accord and conformity (the good boy / good girl attitude)

Example of Interpersonal accord and conformity

Max, a 20-year-old college student who embodies the conventional level of moral reasoning, is studying sociology at a university. He values conformity and adheres to societal norms and expectations when assessing the morality of actions. Max often exhibits the characteristics of the third and fourth stages of moral development.

In interpersonal situations, Max tends to adopt a "good boy/good girl attitude." He strives to maintain positive relationships and seeks approval from others. Max believes that being seen as a responsible and respectful individual is crucial for his social standing and acceptance within his peer group.

For example, when Max's friends invite him to a party where underage drinking is prevalent, he weighs his decision based on societal views and expectations. Although Max personally feels unsure about participating in underage drinking, he considers the pressure to conform to his friends' behavior and fit in with the group. Max believes that conforming to social norms and being seen as a "good boy" will help him maintain his friendships and avoid any potential judgment from his peers.

Similarly, Max demonstrates his conventional moral reasoning when it comes to his academic life. He respects the rules set by his professors and follows the guidelines provided for assignments and exams. Max believes that adhering to these rules is essential for maintaining order and fairness in the academic environment. He avoids cheating or plagiarizing because he understands that it goes against the societal expectation of academic integrity.

Max's decision-making process primarily revolves around societal norms and the desire to conform to them. He places a significant emphasis on being viewed as a responsible and well-behaved individual by others. As a college student at the conventional level of moral reasoning, Max's actions are heavily influenced by interpersonal accord and conformity, reflecting the good boy/good girl attitude commonly associated with this stage of moral development.

2. Authority and social order maintaining orientation (Law and Order morality)

Example of Authority and social order maintaining orientation

Julia, a college student, exemplifies the conventional level of moral reasoning through her adherence to societal views and expectations, particularly in the realm of authority and social order. She displays characteristics of the third and fourth stages of moral development, which revolve around the maintenance of law and order morality. Here's an example illustrating Julia's behavior:

Julia is a diligent and disciplined student who places great value on obeying rules and following established norms. One day, she witnesses her classmates cheating on a test by sharing answers discreetly. While Julia understands that cheating is generally frowned upon and against the rules, she evaluates the situation primarily based on societal expectations and the importancc of maintaining social order.

At the third stage of moral development, Julia's thinking reflects an authority and social order maintaining orientation. She reasons that cheating undermines the fairness of the academic system and jeopardizes the integrity of the test. Julia believes it is her responsibility to uphold the rules and maintain a level playing field for all students.

As a result, Julia decides to confront her classmates privately after the test. She calmly explains to them the negative consequences of cheating, both for themselves and the broader academic community. She encourages them to consider the importance of honesty and hard work in achieving personal growth and fairness for everyone.

In this example, Julia's decision-making process is guided by her conformity to societal norms and her desire to uphold authority and social order. Her moral reasoning is rooted in the conventional level, where actions are evaluated based on societal expectations rather than individual principles or abstract ethical concepts.

Level 3 post conventional

The post conventional level, also known as the principled level, consists of stages 5 and 6 of moral development and realization that individuals are separate entities from society now becomes salient. One's own perspective should be viewed before societies. It is due to this nature of self before others that the post conventional level, especially stage 6, is sometimes mistaken for pre-conventional behaviors.

1. Social contract orientation

Example of Social contract orientation

Theo, a college student in the post-conventional level of moral development, exemplifies the social contract orientation and the realization of individuality and personal perspective as separate from societal norms. He has reached stages 5 and 6 of moral development, which are characterized by a shift in focus from societal expectations to personal values and principles.

Theo believes that individuals have rights and autonomy that should be respected by society. He understands that personal perspectives and values are important and should be considered before conforming to societal expectations. He recognizes that society is made up of diverse individuals with different perspectives, and he values the principles of fairness, justice, and mutual respect.

For example, Theo is involved in student activism on his college campus. When the administration proposes a new policy that he disagrees with, he takes a principled stand based on his personal values and beliefs. He engages in thoughtful discussions and debates with fellow students, faculty, and administrators, advocating for a more inclusive and equitable policy.

Despite societal pressure to conform, Theo remains committed to his principles and the promotion of fairness and social justice. He actively seeks out opportunities to make a positive impact in his community and is willing to challenge authority when he believes it is necessary to uphold his personal values and the rights of others.

It is important to note that the post-conventional level, especially stage 6, can sometimes be mistaken for pre-conventional behaviors. This is because individuals at this stage prioritize their personal perspectives and principles over societal norms, which may appear similar to the self-centeredness of the pre-conventional level. However, the key distinction lies in the fact that individuals in the post-conventional level are guided by principles of fairness, justice, and mutual respect, rather than selfish interests alone.

2. Universal ethical principles

Example of ethical principles

Maya, a college student in the post-conventional level of moral development, exemplifies the principles of stage 5 and stage 6. She has a strong realization that individuals are separate entities from society, and she prioritizes her own perspective before considering societal expectations.

Maya is known among her peers for her unwavering commitment to her personal values and beliefs. She is deeply aware of her individuality and believes that her own judgment and conscience should guide her actions. She critically evaluates societal norms and rules, recognizing that they may not always align with her own ethical principles.

At stage 5, Maya is focused on maintaining social order and adhering to the laws and standards of society. However, she also understands that these norms are not absolute and can be subject to change. Maya recognizes the importance of societal harmony and aims to contribute positively to her community while still maintaining her individuality.

In stage 6, Maya goes beyond the conventional understanding of morality and develops her own universal ethical principles. She firmly believes in the inherent worth and dignity of every individual, valuing justice, equality, and respect for all. Maya's moral compass is guided by principles such as human rights, fairness, and the pursuit of the greater good.

Maya's strong commitment to universal ethical principles might sometimes be misunderstood as pre-conventional behavior. However, her choices and actions are rooted in a deep understanding of the complex nature of moral decision-making. Maya's ability to consider multiple perspectives, weigh the consequences of her actions, and uphold her personal values demonstrates her advanced moral reasoning at the post-conventional level.

Maya's principled stance and her ability to balance her own perspective with societal expectations make her a role model for others in the college community. Her actions reflect a deep sense of individuality, while also showing a commitment to making the world a better place based on universal ethical principles.

Mental Health

[42]Starting in early adolescence, compared with males, females have rates of anxiety that are about twice as high and rates of depression that are 1.5 to 3 times as high (American Psychiatric Association, 2013). Although the rates vary across specific anxiety and depression diagnoses, rates for some disorders are markedly higher in adolescence than in childhood or adulthood. For example, prevalence rates for specific phobias are about 5% in children and 3%–5% in adults but 16% in adolescents. Anxiety and depression are particularly concerning because suicide is one of the leading causes of death during adolescence. Developmental models focus on interpersonal contexts in both childhood and adolescence that foster depression and anxiety (e.g., Rudolph, 2009).

Mental health problems can impact a student's college success. [43]About 58% of students surveyed by *Fortune* reported that emotional or mental difficulties hurt their academic performance last semester. One in five believe their difficulties hurt them a lot.

[44]American college students are facing an unprecedented mental health crisis. Three in five (60%) college students reported being diagnosed with a mental health condition by a professional, the most common afflictions being anxiety and depression, according to an exclusive *Fortune* survey of 1,000 college students conducted by The Harris Poll.

[45]According to college student mental health statistics, around 1,100 US college students commit suicide every year and 24,000 attempt to take their lives.

---

42 www.RISEstudentcoaching.com/resources

43 www.RISEstudentcoaching.com/resources

44 www.RISEstudentcoaching.com/resources

45 www.RISEstudentcoaching.com/resources

College students are exposed to extreme pressure and stress, which negatively impacts their mental health. In the past decade, the number of students treated for mental disorders has been on the rise.

[46]34% of college students have been diagnosed with anxiety (*Healthy Minds Network*). **Due to constant exposure to stress and trauma, many college students in the US are diagnosed with anxiety. To be precise, 34% of students are struggling with this mental health disorder. Of them, 17% have reported severe forms of anxiety, whereas 18% have moderate symptoms. Similar to depression, anxiety has a crippling effect on academic performance.**

One professor shared that depression among white students is widespread and the consequences are dire, "Their silence must be a death unto themselves."

He went on to say, "Most all students self-diagnose with some form of anxiety, OCD, panic attacks, or depression. I'm not saying that students aren't under a lot of stress; they are. What I often observe is that to be in the "in group," students had to exaggerate or focus on their mental health. The culture reinforces students' inability to cope rather than promoting the perspective of overcoming, or being joyful, resilient and adaptable. The university just isn't providing them with structured tools to develop resilience and adaptability.

"It's the norm for students to be 'freaking out' over something, whether it be their classes, a job, no groceries, their parents, their peer group, or a relationship with a significant other. These stressors were amplified by the pressures by the campus culture that encouraged students to question their sexuality, their gender, their values, morals, and beliefs. Although questioning is an integral part of student development at this age, the extreme spectrum of divergent choices

46 www.RISEstudentcoaching.com/resources

pressured students into a mindset of constant contemplation which, in their mind, took on dire urgency; a need to "identify" as something before being called out as someone with no identity group, and worse, a typical stereotypical white, cisgender (denoting or relating to a person whose gender identity corresponds with the sex registered for them at birth; not transgender) middle-class, conservative Christian."

A college student's world is a pressure cooker. In contrast, grown independent adults have a variety of places to go, peer groups to interact with, and interests to pursue. College students are at the narrow point of a funnel. All of their interactions, successes or failures are in the one place that they cannot escape from; college. From this lens, all intersections are at the apex of every day the student is living in, every moment.

Mental health is a significant risk factor for all college students. Studies that research mental health rates specifically of conservative college students are nonexistent; or at least very rare. We can conclude from students' self reporting and college personnel's observation, that conservative students are adversely affected by the hostile campus culture. This makes it imperative that they are offered as much support as possible. Pre-collegiate preparation and ongoing monitoring and check-points are all ways that parents can improve their student's success. Parents need to find methods to establish the development of core competencies such as resilience, and facilitating the evolution of the skills and qualities necessary for success such as:

- Values
- Identity
- Leadership
- Healthy Relationships

- Communication
- Civil engagement and understanding diversity, equity and inclusion, and privilege
- Cultural differences and conflict resolution
- Academic resourcefulness

RISE Student Coaching is a resource that can be extremely valuable in supporting your student's development and enhancing the skills they need to maintain strong mental health. Implementing a powerful plan, and enlisting your own support staff can make the difference between success and failure, struggle and peace of mind, joy and pain, and health or illness.

CHAPTER 5

Student Support

PEER GROUP

Sarah's work study was perfect this year. She got to work in the library, which meant she got paid to study. Her job was to verify the condition of microfiche in the basement. After completing a couple of drawers, she would retreat to the study desk in the corner and unpack her bag. She'd been told by her supervisor she had the entire semester to complete the project, and was welcome to manage her time as she wished.

This year was going great. She loved her new apartment and her roommates had been pretty good so far. Braced for drama, Sarah was relieved that there wasn't more controversy than things like dirty dishes left in the sink.

At the end of her shift, Sarah closed her laptop and climbed up the creaking ancient stairs to the main floor. It was late and the library was closing for the day. Sarah stopped and asked another student worker if she needed help with anything while locking up. No, they were almost done.

Walking through the lobby, Sarah was stopped by a small group of students. They asked if she was "The Republican." Huh? Sarah was taken aback and wasn't sure what this was about. A blonde, blue-eyed guy spoke for the group. They knew who she was and what she stood for. They were all insulted by her opinions. Speechless, Sarah stood in front of them feeling her heartbeat race and adrenaline beginning to pump through her. "You'd better watch your back," she was told. They all turned and walked through the glass doors into the night.

Fumbling with her cell phone, Sarah tapped "Mom" on the screen. The phone rolled to VoiceMail, evidently shut off for the night. She knew her Dad's phone would be on, but she really didn't want to talk to him about this right now.

Alone, Sarah walked across the library lawn to the dimly lit parking lot. Her uneasiness grew the farther she moved from the library. Could they have been serious? Was that a real threat? Her body screamed that it was, while her mind tried to rationalize that it wasn't. How could they know? The only thing Sarah could recall was, while eating breakfast with her roommates, agreeing aloud with a political news report about a bill that senate republicans were planning to veto. Sarah felt, for the first time on her campus, alone and afraid of everyone.

Peer group influence can have a major impact on college students. Peers may encourage or discourage behaviors that are beneficial or harmful to the student's academic success and overall well being. For example, peers may influence the amount of time a student spends studying and attending class, their involvement in extracurricular activities, and even their lifestyle choices. It is important for college students to be aware of how peer group influences can shape their decisions and recognize potential disparities between themselves and the group they identify with. By understanding these differences, students can make informed decisions about who they choose as friends and mentors during their college experience. Conservative students are faced with an additional layer of challenges when it comes to peer group influence. They must work to seek out like-minded conservative peers and risk being ostracized by the large majority of progressive students, or conform to fit in. These are difficult but critical decisions students face. A game-plan prior to leaving for college is useful in determining a healthy pathway to social fulfillment.

It is essential for faculty members to create learning environments that foster positive relationships among peers so that all students feel comfortable sharing ideas. In nearly all classes, students are required to work in groups on projects, research, or presentations. In some instances the groups are self created, other instances the instructor assigns groups. The goal of the educator is to allow students the ability to gain skills and experience in communication, project management, public speaking, negotiation, time management, and accountability, as a representation of real-life work situations. Students oftentimes report the frustration of learning in these groups. If a student has been recognized in class for being a conservative, which is viewed by their peers as being different and unwanted, and left with no support, working within these groups may be very difficult and a challenge. To create cohesion with this peer group to allow them all to participate equally, faculty have the perfect opportunity to create strong and healthy working relationships within these work groups. It's reported, though, that this opportunity is being missed and perhaps even a hostile environment is being created by progressive instructors making it very difficult for conservative students to participate and thrive in this peer group environment.

[47]This is why 55.1% of Republicans don't tell their friends about their political views. Republicans on campus are nearly 4x more likely to hide their political views from their friends than Democrats. The fear of being cast with damning labels and feeling ostracized is a genuine fear for conservatives on campus. It's also why 55.1% of Republicans are

47 www.RISEstudentcoaching.com/resources

closet conservatives who don't tend to share their political orientation with their friends.

For Democrats, being part of a college campus that mostly shares their views could be what contributes to feeling accepted in inner and wider circles.

[48]A new poll from NBC News that looked at second-year college and university students is generating attention after revealing that "nearly half of college students wouldn't room with someone who votes differently." More specifically, the poll found that 54 percent of sophomores would "definitely" or "probably" be open to living with someone who supported the presidential candidate they opposed in 2020, but 46 percent said they would "probably not" or "definitely not."

There is an assumption that people think the way they do. Describing his experience, one student said, "If people were willing to accept that there are differing views on campus, that would be kind of nice." [49]According to research from the Pew Research Center, liberals are more likely to unfriend you over politics - online and offline. It shows Republicans and Democrats share very different social lives on campus. Republicans have to suppress their voice to feel accepted, while Democrats can speak without thinking twice.

[50]One conservative student flatly declared that his opinions were "not acceptable" on campus. "I've rarely felt comfortable expressing my own views," the student wrote. "When I first expressed them, word got around my college house and I was quickly excommunicated and constantly avoided by most residents."

48 www.RISEstudentcoaching.com/resources

49 www.RISEstudentcoaching.com/resources

50 www.RISEstudentcoaching.com/resources

Victoria shared her experience with peers. "All students want to fit in. Students tend to want to be what the other students want them to be. That's comfortable to be the same as everyone else. When I was at a super conservative campus I tried to fit in. When I went to a more liberal campus I tried to fit in there, too. Living in the dorms is so hard. Whether you're on a liberal campus or a conservative, living on campus, it's so intense. You just want to make friends. You just want to fit in and maybe find a boyfriend.

"I found myself just wanting to run away from my problems. I didn't find any support or any help anywhere on campus. I was just alone. I wish I had been more prepared before I got on campus. I wish I had understood what it would be like, or someone would have told me how to make friends, or how to be ready for the classes that I was going to be in. I just thought it was going to be a lot of fun and everyone would get along. That's what the campus told me before I got there and I believed them. But that's just not the truth.

"My parents have both been to college, but it was so different for them. Kids really need someone to coach them or tell them how to get along on campuses today, how to live in the dorms, or how to go to the dining hall and not feel isolated there in a group of people. It wasn't healthy that I quit eating because I hated the dining halls so bad; it only made things worse for me. I found that I had two problems on my hands. I was struggling in classes. I was trying to make friends. I was isolating and getting more and more depressed while I steadily lost weight and felt weaker. And it was harder to concentrate and to study. There really shouldn't be politics in education anymore. But who's trying to stop it?

"Students who have been public about pro-life opinions have been targeted and bullied. Their displays, posters and information have been torn down and ruined. When they have tried to speak with those of opposing views about why they support abortions, few students have really been able to answer the questions. They answer with statements such as, 'Well, because that's just not right, *women's body women's choice.*' That PR campaign has been so successful. Students can't articulate why they believe in pro-choice because they're not allowed to have conversations about it. They are simply required to swallow the party line and regurgitate it when anyone asks. All they can do is repeat the same propaganda that they have been exposed to and told that this is the correct answer. You're a 'cool kid' or acceptable if this is your response to these difficult questions."

What happens to these students whose identity is developing? What's happening to these students whose moral values, their social mores, their worldview is so pliable and flexible at this time of their life and they're only offered one point of view or one belief system?

At a small rural university, 7% of the student population are students of color. Most students are white and from the surrounding area of the state. But the campus has designated a number of "zones" all over campus that are for students of color only, such as bulletin boards that are "Diversity, Inclusion, and Equity (DIE) Boards," but white students are not allowed to post bulletins there, whether or not the content is related to DIE or not. Students have to walk through the DIE office to get food donated to the student food pantry. The atmosphere is conspicuously unwelcoming to white students. In both of these instances, the perceived needs of a small percentage of the student population drives administration to make decisions that exclude the white students for no other reason than to placate the woke activists on campus.

Curiously, many students of color don't want segregation. Students in a discussion group on a very liberal east coast campus expressed sadness and confusion over the campus climate. They see that white privilege does exist in many circumstances, but not all, and felt it was sad that anyone should have to apologize for their whiteness.

Immigrants from Africa, India, and Asia, and many other countries deemed in the US to be "brown" or "of color" consider it a benefit to study and work beside their white peers. Their stories are often very similar. Their parents were dedicated to formally immigrating to the United States solely to give their children a better life with endless opportunities. Those parents work two or three jobs to provide their children with an American life, despite having had higher social or economic status in their native country. These students and their families desire to have multi-racial, multicultural peer groups. Their dream and sacrifice, in so many cases, has been precisely to provide for their children opportunities to work and get to know American students of every race and ethnicity, and certainly not to have white American students ostracized and compromised.

Conservative students joining tight-knit groups such as the arts, theater, fraternities, or sororities soon find that their opinions are out of line and therefore they are not welcome. In-group and out-group dynamics are quickly established. Greek organizations were historically conservative and elite. Their selection process was subjective and only those students that were deemed to be a "fit" to the mission of the fraternity were selected. An amazing shift has occurred over the past few years. Sororities are now openly requesting the resignation of members that are openly conservative. Liberal-leaning members are resigning voluntarily in protest of the organization's past discriminatory history. The primary purpose of Greek institutions on campuses is to connect peer groups and create lifelong friendships. Even within Greek societies, in-group and out-group dynamics have been established.

Tabling is an established form of communication and recruitment and establishes commonality for students on campus. Any group has the ability to publicly table. They go to the office at the Student Union or the office of student involvement, they fill out a form and application and staff or administration will consider the application and its merit. The staff will either approve or deny the application. Anyone who has not gone through the application process and approval will be asked to leave by the university. It is considered controlled and there are established guidelines and rules that students must adhere to in order to table what they can and cannot communicate, how they can communicate, how they can approach other students including what kind of language they can use. Everything is clearly defined prior to tabling. It's very well established and students know the rules.

Mike, one of the students that I interviewed who was attending a large campus, was tabling during the Trump campaign in 2016 and was placed across from students tabling for Black Lives Matter. The students at both tables were respectful to each other, but they didn't interact much. They were following the guidelines and the rules that the university had set out for tabling behavior. They were simply talking to the students that were interested in what they had to say and greeted the other students that were passing by. "There was a lot of yelling at us and name calling all day. Groups of students would see us and one would start and then the other would join in as they passed."

A group of students stopped at the BLM table and then turned around and approached the students at the Trump table. Name calling ensued. The students tabling for Trump found it difficult, but necessary to maintain control of the situation and not react. Mike said that the women working at the Trump campaign table felt very threatened because the "BLM group" was very aggressive, yelling in their faces. "They were yelling at the women and the guys were stepping in and saying, 'Hey man, talk to us instead. Stop yelling at them.' The "BLM group" finally backed away and left."

When they went home at the end of the day, they walked in a large group dropping off the women first, worried for their safety. Once home alone, the impact of the day and being subjected to so much hate speech took its toll. The students were exhausted emotionally and mentally. Where do they go for support? Parents, of course. But at the university level, support is not provided for these students. It is the belief of the students involved that if the roles were reversed and students that had stopped by their table and then crossed over and began heckling the Black Lives Matter students something would have been done. It would have been reported and the university would have taken action.

A few days later while hanging up Trump posters on a public bulletin board, Mike was approached by another student saying, "You can't put that here!" Mike turned around to face the students and said, "It's a student bulletin board. I'm allowed to put it here, and I'm allowed to have my opinions and to state them publicly!" A mob started gathering around them. The group was yelling, "Black people are being killed in the streets and that's genocide!" Mike has nothing to do with black people being killed in the streets, but it was perceived that because he's hanging up Trump signs that he was partly responsible. The student aggressor got closer, hit the sign with his fist and said, "What are you going to do about that?" He dropped his backpack and threatened Mike who was again putting up the sign. "I'll beat the s*** out of you, you f****** clowns!" Another student who was with Mike was recording the altercation on his phone so it was all documented.

The students that were attacked and threatened reported it to campus administration. They requested to speak to the president of the University to talk about threats and violence on campus and that conservative students were feeling unsafe. The president of the campus would not talk to them. He instead sent out a statement to the campus reiterating the policies of nonviolence and left it at that. There was no pursuit of action against the threatening students, not even restorative justice. It feels to conservative students on campus that there is no justice for them, and their peers are allowed to try to provoke or intimidate them at their whim.

All of these competing messages and institutional barriers make true connections between students nearly insurmountable. They are forced to navigate around the maze of misinformation and institutional bias to find and speak to one another. Once introductions are satisfactorily accepted, students then must cross the troubled waters of prejudgment, prejudice, and indoctrination. All of these barriers were created by society and institutions. Students are now facing the racial gulf intentionally constructed to divide them. Systemic bias does exist! It is as flagrant now as it was in the '50s and '60s, only it is in opposition to white students.

Understandably, students are reluctant to speak out or stick their neck out for their beliefs, morals or values. The risk of loss is too great. Knowing the reality of the rejection by their peers leaves them few options.

Peer groups in college are not significantly unlike the peer groups students leave in high school. Their peer group selection becomes more sophisticated as students mature. Their focus is different, their needs may be different, but the strength of acceptance by their peers is just as strong as it was the year before college.

Students come to campus believing that they will fit in. They believe that they will find their like-minded friends and even potentially their life partners. Unfortunately, that's a difficult path to navigate. Oftentimes their introduction to friends is their roommate in the dorms or the other students on their floor. They cluster together at the beginning of the year. They eat together, they study together and friend groups pair off.

Creating a strategy before going to college ensures that the student will find a supportive peer group if they follow the process. Identifying affinity groups both on-campus and off, and including it in their college-prep plan with specific information including contacts, locations, and a timeline immensely improves a student's odds at finding a suitable peer group. Peer group influence is strong in all human beings. The adversarial campus climate and peer rejection can begin to seep into a student's self-identity. So when faced with these tough choices of fitting in or being left out, students will oftentimes conform to the peer group and abandon their own identity, morals and values.

COMMUNITY

Finding a sense of community in college is essential for success. It can provide a much-needed support system and encourage an individual to pursue their academic, social, and career goals. Fortunately, there are plenty of opportunities to connect with peers on campus through clubs, organizations, and other activities.

The first step is to look into what the school offers. Many colleges have student organizations that range from academics to hobbies or special interests. Joining one—or more—of these groups can help build meaningful relationships with people who share similar values and experiences. Additionally, attending events hosted by the university or groups is another great way to get involved and meet new people.

Another option is to utilize online resources like Instagram groups or Reddit to learn about what's going on in and around campus. Online groups also offer an opportunity to connect with students at other universities. A coaching network or app offers students instant connections to other students around topics or concerns. Apps, like the "Rise Student Coaching" app, provide community features.

Off-campus opportunities abound in college towns. Searching local groups and organizations related to student interests can help them find events where they can make genuine connections with other people in the area.

Finding a sense of community takes time and effort. With all of the available options, there's bound to be something out there that will help foster a deeper connection with others so that students can feel at home in their college environment. By exploring all these opportunities, students can quickly make friends and build a positive support system that will help them throughout their college experience.

Building community is the foundation of college life, second only to academic achievement.

Community is more broad than a peer group of students and offers a sense of belonging and identity. For conservative students, it is especially important for them to find a community to connect with in order to feel that they are engaged in something greater than themselves as individuals and that people are counting on them and value them. Community provides an opportunity for them to grow and develop their skills to become contributing members of their future communities.

It can't be stressed enough how important this foundation is to the development of college students, giving them a sense of purpose and providing a pathway for engagement and successful relationships and enterprise. This paves the way for adulthood, providing opportunities to learn how to engage in the broader community and to develop a sense of responsibility to prioritize civic engagement. Whether it be a theater group, athletic team, or a volunteer organization, building community is essential for college students to find balance and structure that allows them to grow and feel confident.

GETTING BY GIVING

A student development theory by Alexander Aston identifies that the role of student involvement in development and for growth and learning to occur students must be engaged in their environment. The amount of student learning and personal development is directly proportional to the quality and quantity of student involvement. The more students put into an activity, the more they get out of it.

It's well documented that what we see and what we hear around us highly influences our perspective of the world. It changes our choices, our perceptions, and our understanding of the world around us. Take for example the recent happenings of centuries old statues being torn down in cities and town squares across the country. An interpretation or belief held by some, is that they represented racism, misogyny and discrimination. It was not taken into consideration the other side, the true side, the balanced understanding of these centuries old figures and what they stood for; if nothing else, they stood for and represented history - even the dark sides of our history. We, as citizens of this country, have a right and an obligation to understand all of our history, both good and bad. Especially our children. Our children need to know what we as human beings are capable of.

Reading through the Bible, especially the Old Testament, one finds countless examples of abhorrent behavior; all representative of human nature, the nature of humaneness. The same is true for the Koran and the Torah. Ancient writings offer a valuable gift; an insight into the range of human experience. The fact that the Bible has existed for thousands of years and Christianity has survived as a central religion on our planet is testament to the fact that the stories and the lessons learned are universal throughout written history, time, and throughout cultures. It spans from language to language and generation to generation. It represents us as human beings.

Tearing down our statues and the opportunity for our youth and young adults to consider the impact of historical events is devastating to our future. Generations need to have the opportunity to review and reflect on decisions and choices made by leaders within the context of their time and culture. Taking historical situations out of context and placing them into our 21st century sensibilities is nonsense. We have an opportunity to learn, but that is not what's happening. Our children are being indoctrinated. The next generation is being brainwashed to believe that in isolation our national leaders were evil; they were not. They are *not* being taught a worldview through the lens of time and history, and synthesizing the varied factors including geography, economics, human development, culture, psychology and understanding of humaneness. Separating these factors completely from one another and considering only 'the one' that supports the popular philosophy of the moment does not serve our students or the future of our society. Separating ourselves from one another because of these philosophies will eventually destroy the foundation of our homes, communities, and our country.

Separating ourselves from one another can never end well. Individually and collectively we need to be engaged with each other and our world. Fear has permeated our culture. Students fear offending others at every turn. We'll serve our students and the world by connecting and becoming a part of the whole, rather than separating ourselves from it.

Like the historical statues, we can't allow students to be intimidated and retreat because it is the judgment of some that they are of no value. We need to lead the way and show students how to connect with each other and the whole world, the good, the bad, and the ugly. The more connected they are to the world by giving, serving and engaging, the stronger individuals they will be, and the stronger our society will be. How to change others' worldview or opinions is beyond the scope of this book; that might take volumes. But it is possible to develop strategies and methods to show young adults that by engaging, giving, volunteering and becoming part of the community, they get back as much or more than they give. We can't allow fear to hold them back.

We have to serve as champions and role models to show them how to march forward and take their place in the community.

Getting students out of their own head and their dorm rooms and out into the community working with others and volunteering is the best antidote available for self doubt and anxiety. It gives them an opportunity to stretch and grow as others benefit from their time and commitment. It develops many of the skills necessary to move forward in life.

Some of the benefits of volunteering include:

1) *It improves mental health and well-being.*

   Volunteering has been shown to help reduce and counteract the negative effects of stress, anger and anxiety which can lead to depression and substance abuse. Community service offers opportunities to engage in social interactions and helps to uplift others, making a positive impact and becoming part of something bigger than themselves.

2) *Helping others.* It's rewarding and enriching to help others. Volunteering gives students the opportunity to give their time and talents to support something that's important to them. Giving back also illustrates to students their own impact on others and the world. When they pause and reflect on their work, they understand their value in the bigger world as they contribute to others.

3) *Networking opportunities.* Networking is now one of the most important ways for students to begin to make the segue into the career world. By volunteering in a group, students are able to meet and work with students who share common interests and expand their overall network of diverse mentors and peers.

4) *They gain experience they can use on a resume.* By being involved in community service, students are able to apply their in-class education to real world scenarios with real impacts. They develop key career experience in leadership, time management, and problem solving, all which lead to greater confidence during the job search and interview.

5) *Build self-esteem and confidence.* The more often students are given opportunities to safely expand their comfort zone, the farther they grow and the more confident they become to go out into the world to apply for jobs, to interview for jobs, and to begin a career of their own.

In a world filled with negativity and decisiveness, it's imperative that students continue to stretch and grow. Volunteering and service learning is one of the best ways to combat the negativity of the world around them and to contribute to something worthwhile, and help themselves along the way. Learning to tune out the radical judgments and values and tune in to one's own internal compass is a valuable outcome of volunteering and service learning.

Students can find appropriate placements on campus, through local community centers, or through your RISE Student Coach. Whichever avenue you choose, allow students to be a part of the process and take the lead by choosing where they'd like to go, what they'd like to do and to complete the application process. A benefit of working with a RISE Student Coach is that students will expand their learning by providing reflection opportunities and transform the experience into true service learning. Service learning is driven by learning objectives and assessments may also be submitted for course credit, in some instances.

CHAPTER 6

Strategies

COACHING

Coaching is different from tutoring or therapy. Empowering the client is the principal objective of coaching. The client holds the power and the direction of the coaching process. The client establishes their own objectives and together, with the leadership of the coach, the client and the coach develop a pathway to achieving their goals. The coach serves as an accountability partner, a guide, and a resource to move through the steps to success and the achievement of their goals.

The elements of coaching are:

- *Establishing the Goal.* The beginning of any coaching interaction needs to start with a clear purpose. The professional standard method for goal setting is following the SMART GOAL format.
    - SPECIFIC: Goals should be distinct and explicit. The more narrow the goal, the easier it will be to focus on and strategize for execution.

  - MEASUREABLE: Define goals with specific criteria that measure your progress toward the accomplishment of the goal. Measurable goals ensure successes and personal inspiration along the way.
  - ACHIEVABLE: Goals should be challenging and visionary, but not impossible to achieve. If not realistically achievable, the goal will lead to defeat.
  - REALISTIC: The goal should be relevant to your life and consistent with your undertaking.
  - TIMELY: Have a clearly defined timeline, including a starting date and a target date. The purpose is to create urgency.

- *Understanding through Assessment.* Periodic assessments will be conducted throughout the coaching process. This can be as simple as an audit or review of the smart goals, or can be more complex with deeper insight to determine where strengths and weaknesses lie and to revise goals accordingly.
- *Providing Feedback.* Coaching is much more than listening or checking in. A coach will provide regular feedback, research support options and resources, and offer suggestions for improvement.
- *Following up with Support.* Throughout the coaching process, the coach will offer support. Phone calls, text messages, Zoom meetings, or other touch-points will be available to the client. Achievement of the goals, or the conclusion of the coaching period may not end the coaching relationship. The coach may periodically offer check-in opportunities.

Most people are familiar, either through firsthand experience or watching films or movies with scenes of traditional therapy, how the client talks to the therapist, the therapist parrots back what the client has said, and through a lengthy process of gentle guidance the client may eventually resolve their issues and establish new patterns of behavior. This process has been proven very effective for many types of mental maladies, emotional fatigue, and tragic phases of one's life.

Coaching takes on a different role for students. Therapy is beneficial for many students, and coaching does not replace mental health intervention. When it comes to college students, coaching offers distinct advantages over traditional talk therapy. First, coaching is action-oriented and goal-focused, making it particularly beneficial for students who are seeking practical strategies to navigate the challenges of college life. Coaching helps students set clear objectives, develop effective study habits, manage time efficiently, and enhance their overall academic performance. Unlike talk therapy, which may delve into deep-rooted emotional issues, coaching primarily concentrates on providing tangible solutions and support to address specific challenges. Secondly, coaching for college students often incorporates mentorship and guidance, allowing them to benefit from the experience and expertise of their coaches. Coaches can provide valuable insights on career planning, internship opportunities, and job search strategies, which are crucial for college students transitioning into the professional world. Additionally, coaching offers regular check-ins and accountability, helping students stay motivated, focused, and on track towards achieving their academic and personal goals. Overall, coaching empowers college students with practical tools, actionable advice, and personalized support to thrive during their college years and beyond.

RISE Student Coaching

Resilience and Independence Skills for Engagement

[51]With *only 45% of students graduating from college*, the United States' graduation rate lags behind that of most developed countries. According to the Organization for Economic Cooperation and Development (OECD), U.S. college graduation rates rank 19th out of the 28 countries studied.

Several key factors are responsible for student attrition; a feeling of isolation, difficulty adjusting to a new environment, and an inability to integrate new information and knowledge with previous information and knowledge. As students transition into college during their freshman year, especially, weaving social and academic integration into the fabric of their university experience is critical.

RISE is a cohort-based student development program that brings together students from across the country to learn from and support each other while moving through the RISE Engagement Strategies. The RISE Student Coaching program is based upon research authenticating the importance of mastering resilience skills, as well as learning coping and engagement skills. Resilience allows students to adapt and change through difficult and trying experiences. Engagement skills move students forward through their development allowing them to continue to grow and develop with confidence while interacting with their peers, developing leadership skills, academic focus, developing and maintaining community engagement, and understanding global engagement skills.

---

51 www.RISEstudentcoaching.com/resources

The RISE Student Coaching program is built on the 5 pillars of engagement:

- Resilience Skills
- Personal Engagement
- Community Engagement
- Global Engagement
- Academic Engagement

These 5 pillars of engagement enable students to leave their college experience stronger and more prepared for life as they continue to develop and grow. These foundational blocks prepare students to be leaders not only in their own lives and community, but also in the world.

Resilience

Research has shown that several skills must be used to be successful in college. One of those skills is resilience. Resilience is a life skill that is acquired in youth and developed over a lifetime. Goal setting is, of course, necessary to navigate the rigorous curriculum to successfully graduate from college. But, without resilience, students lack the ability to stay the course when they have fallen short of their goals. Bouncing back, getting back on the horse, and looking for the silver lining is typical advice given to those needing to rely on their resilience.

When someone bounces back from setbacks and continues to thrive, they are said to be resilient. But resilience is easier said than done. Resilience is a learned skill and one that can be intentionally developed over time. Resilience is our ability to adapt well and recover quickly following experiences of stress, adversity, trauma or tragedy. If you have a resilient disposition, you are better able to maintain wellness in the face of life's challenges. If you're less resilient, you're more likely to dwell on problems, feel overwhelmed, use unhealthy coping tactics to handle stress, and develop anxiety and depression.

It's a life skill that is critical for students to develop before and throughout college. Our K-12 public schools, however, have negated many of the opportunities to build resilience in children as they move through school years. It's become unfashionable and intolerable for a student to suffer disappointment, not win a trophy, left to feel different, or even to simply feel sad. It's been a difficult process for parents to navigate as the culture has developed into one that, if you leave your child to rely on their own developing sense of self, their own resilience, you are deemed a bad parent. It's been established that children in our culture should never be permitted to feel sorrowful or distressed. How then does a child build resilience skills? How then does a child develop into a functioning adult who can cope with the inevitable ups and downs of life? It's impossible without practice. It's impossible without guidance. Parents have been backed into a corner and led to believe it's just not right.

A strong RISE Student Coaching program based on child development and accompanied by solid parenting practices can support parents as their children grow and develop through their K-12 years, and into their collegiate careers. The RISE Student Coaching program offsets the gaslighting that's happening in our public education system today, and supports and collaborates with parents and students.

Parents and students preparing for college, and those that are already enrolled and navigating the university system, are benefited by finding and utilizing a great RISE coach. Resilience is defined as the capacity to recover quickly from difficulties. Building resilience in students and young adults is highly effective in a coaching environment.

Assisting parents through RISE Student Coaching to build their parenting skills during those unique and very challenging adolescent and young adult years is a very effective way to bolster parents in their support and guidance of their students. A key component of RISE Student Coaching for parents is building a trusting community. Essential to developing confidence is nurturing a strong voice with which to communicate. Sharing resources is another cornerstone of a coaching community. A benefit of our technological culture is that reaching out and building community is almost effortless if one is committed to developing their strength and confidence.

Finding and utilizing available resources such as webinars, online Zoom communities and meetings, apps, and in-person retreats and workshops are all resources that will develop one's skills and build their confidence so that parents and students will navigate the challenges of higher education with ease.

Resilience skills are applied to countless life situations and are the foundation to the RISE Student Coaching program. Fostering resilience applies to a myriad of life situations students and parents may face such as workplace challenges, natural disasters, and leadership struggles, family dynamics, learning mindfulness or a religious practice, developing mental endurance, sports competition, academics, psychology, parenting, being a specific group such as a military family or immigrants from another country and culture.

Resilience skills hold an individual firmly in place when hardship strikes. We are less likely to abandon our own values and beliefs and can stand firmly and triumphantly until difficult times have passed. Coaching provides the tools to build resilience so parents and students flourish throughout their lives.

Kenneth Ginsburg, MD, has done extensive research on resilience in parents and teens. Dr. Ginsburg is a pediatrician specializing in Adolescent Medicine at the Children's Hospital of Philadelphia, a

Professor of Pediatrics at the University of Pennsylvania School of Medicine, and Co-Founder and Director of Programs at Center for Parent and Teen Communication. Dr. Ginsburg has identified "7 C's of Resilience."

The 7 C's of Resilience for parents and teens, by Kenneth Ginsburg, MD

1. Competence
2. Confidence
3. Connection
4. Character
5. Contribution
6. Coping
7. Control

The American Psychological Association outlines four core components of resilience:

- Connection
- Wellness
- Healthy thinking
- Meaning

Focusing on these four core components will empower students to withstand and learn from difficult and traumatic experiences. Resilience research began at the University of Minnesota and was founded by developmental psychologist Norman Garmezy, who led "*Project Competence,*" a longitudinal study at the University of

Minnesota. Along with other researchers, Garmezy developed the resilience theory by studying, over a number of years, the difference between patients with mental illness who successfully improved with resilience skills and those who failed to improve,; who had limited resilience skills or underdeveloped skills. It's been shown over time that deliberate attention to and development of resilience skills builds strong and thriving adults who can recover from difficulties, failures and disappointments.

Resilience is defined as the capacity to withstand or to recover quickly from difficulties. Adversity is as much a part of the life experience as is success and ease. Resilience is a learned skill that is developed throughout our life experience, beginning in childhood and developing throughout one's entire life. World calamities, personal calamities, anxiety, stress, high expectations, disappointments, and failures are all opportunities to grow as individuals. These opportunities offer us the foundational blocks on which we grow; each failure or disappointment is a stepping stone on which we proceed to further growth and further ability to withstand life's difficulties. Without the opportunity for children and young adults to experience these stumbling blocks, they are unable to build the stepping stones for the foundation of life success that's built on resilience.

Many parents with great intentions and a huge heart and adoration for their children protect them and prevent them from the opportunities to build resilience. Few parents find it easy to see their children cry or be in pain. In fact, as they grow into adulthood that becomes even harder for parents to endure. The risks are greater and the disappointments are harder. By protecting children from the hardships of the world and of life they, in fact, hobble them. A coaching program that focuses on resilience can build children up and develop the skills they need to be successful in college.

Mixed messages in our society have left parents unsure how to navigate parenting their teens and young adults. It is commonplace in higher education to hear professionals refer to incoming freshmen as the maturational equivalent of a 15-year-old of a decade or two ago rather than a budding adult of 18 or 19 years old. Attributing this to the student's "maturity level" is a nebulous term. More helpful and precise is to discuss maturity levels in terms of development and resilience. Resilience skills also overlap with the stages of transition development as published by Schlossberg's transition theory, *"The Four S's: Four major factors that influence a person's ability to cope in transition."*

This transition theory outlines:

Situation: Triggering and timing of a situation

- Person's control
- If situation causes a role change
- Duration
- Previous experience with transitions
- Concurrent stress and assessment of transition

Self: Personal and demographic characters affecting how an individual views life

- Psychological resources that aid with coping with transition
- Socioeconomic status
- Gender
- Ethnicity/Culture
- Age

- Stage of life
- Health

Support: Type, function and measurement of support

- Intimate relationships
- Family units
- Networks of friends
- Institutions
- Communities
- Professional intervention

Strategies: Ability to cope or modify the situation

- Those that control the meaning of the problem
- Those that aid in managing the stress in the aftermath
- Information seeking
- Direct action
- Inhibition of action
- Intrapsychic behavior

PATHWAY TO RISE STUDENT COACHING SUCCESS

"The Seven C's of Resilience" and "The Four S's" of Schlossberg transition theory map out the pathway to coaching success for students and parents navigating College. This allows them to build up their resources to a level that they can successfully withstand the adverse culture of college campuses today.

Building resilience through coaching means the difference between struggle and success for students in our "woke" universities. Building resilience through coaching for parents means the end of sleepless nights, the dark sense of being alone, and the ability to rise to the occasion in order to successfully support one's student in times of difficulty and challenge.

The RISE Student Coaching Program focuses on resilience and the development of life skills including engagement personally, within the community, globally, and academically. The coaching program is designed to teach students resilience skills, resourcefulness, and self-reliance. Opportunities are built into the program to engage with the community which can be defined as friendships, a college community, a life or neighborhood community, and the global community.

RISE Student Coaching Program Overview

Resilience Development

a. Competence
b. Confidence
c. Connection
d. Character
e. Contribution
f. Coping
g. Control

Personal Engagement

a. Values Development
b. Identity Development

c. Leadership Development

Community Engagement

a. Healthy Relationships

b. Communication Skill Building

c. Diversity, Equity, Inclusion

d. Service

Global Engagement

a. Dimensions of Culture

b. Intercultural Communication

c. Cultural Conflict Styles

Academic Engagement

a. Self-Advocacy Development

b. Time Management

c. Resource Identification

d. Academic and Career Planning

Personal engagement is a student's growing ability to engage with themselves. This skill set allows students to fully identify their values. What do they believe in, and what are their morals? They have opportunities to evaluate their values from various points of view and life scenarios, and to boil them down to a core group of values that they can use throughout their life to make assessments and decisions.

Within *personal engagemen*t students also have opportunities to explore their identity. This identity examination is useful as they make decisions in their life such as career choices or long-term relationships. Using assessment tools such as the Myers-Briggs and the Enneagram, students find ways to explore their identity and be able to personally monitor and measure their development and growth.

Personal engagement also encompasses leadership development. Every student, whether they're an introvert or an extrovert, regardless how they've seen themselves previously in comparison to their peers, all have leadership abilities. RISE Student Coaching guides them through a process to identify what their leadership skills are and how best they can apply them. Using the Student Leadership Challenge, they can bring out their innate natural leadership skills and identify the ways that they can apply them.

Community engagement concentrates on communication skills. To be a contributing and vibrant member of any community, one must have developed effective communication skills. Communication skills modules teach how to have difficult conversations, listening skills, public speaking, and the ability to speak one's own truth with confidence and ease. Within the context of a progressive campus, and society, it is critical for our students to develop their communication skills and have the confidence to define and defend their positions in life whether it be political, spiritual, religious, or personal.

Community engagement also allows students to explore healthy relationships. They will discover patterns of behavior, assumptions and expectations they have of others and themselves, and find ways to identify relationships that are healthy and helpful and how to nurture them.

Community engagement explores diversity, equity and inclusion (DIE) including white privilege. Although progressive campus culture has allowed DIE to consume most of the curriculum on campus, it can still be explored through the lens of a traditional or conservative student. Exploring DIE in a safe environment with other like-minded students and a RISE Student Coach provides an ability to be honest and truthful with oneself and others, and to truly come out on the other side with the tools necessary to navigate the work world with confidence and the experience of deep self-reflection and humility.

Global engagement is based on the work of Mitch Hammer, Ph.D., who developed the Intercultural Development Inventory, the Intercultural Development Continuum, and the Intercultural Conflict Styles model and assessment. Students will explore the dimensions of culture and intercultural communication. Culture is a fundamental cause of conflict and misunderstanding between individuals. Students will not only be able to view global relationships through the lens of culture, but they will be able to view personal and intimate relationships through the lens of cultural differences. This offers them the tools to navigate life with better communication and insight.

Academic engagement may assist students in developing skills to seek out and utilize resources such as tutors, TAs, and professors. Oftentimes students may be aware of the resources they have available, but are unwilling and intimidated to go and use these resources. Self-advocacy skills will prepare them to speak confidently and clearly and to communicate to their professors and instructors what their needs are when they need assistance. Time management is also a critical skill that is imperative in order to achieve academic success. Individuals have very unique time management tendencies and habits and those will be explored through RISE Student Coaching to establish the most effective methods for each student.

RISE Coaching for Parents

Case study, Angela and Todd.

Angela is happily married with three teenage and young adult children. Noah, her oldest, was accepted to the Oklahoma State University, his father's alma mater. The family celebrated and were thrilled for Noah. Noah left for his first semester filled with excitement and confidence. Angela tearfully waved good-bye as they drove away. Noah proudly stood on the steps of his residence hall with his hands shoved in his pockets and nodded back at her, grinning broadly. When Noah came home for Thanksgiving break, he was a different person. Although she detected changes in him during their phone conversations, he reported that he was doing well at OU. Once home, he appeared depressed, withdrawn, and troubled. After days of gentle probing, Angela and Todd discovered that he had a hard time fitting in. Everywhere he went he was bombarded with politically correct language, socially progressive ideology, shaming messages for being a white Christian male, and countless other things, like being forced to acknowledge and accept that he had to announce his preferred pronouns in every campus setting. His stories were shocking to Angela and Todd. Surely, his academic advisor, his RA, his Hall Director could offer guidance and support. No, he had tried all of those avenues, and was again and again chastised for not accepting the prevailing liberal campus philosophy.

Angela and Todd prevented Noah from dropping out of OU, and stumbled along through his first year with no guidance for themselves or for Noah. It was a strain on their marriage. Jesse, their second child, is a junior in high school and is hoping to be accepted to the University of Nebraska. Angela is committed to avoiding the nightmare they experienced with Noah, and supports Jesse earning a degree from a well-respected public institution. She will go to any length to ensure his academic, personal, and spiritual success while attending University of Nebraska-Lincoln.

When I first spoke with Angela about the RISE Student Coaching Program, I asked her about her fears for Jesse. She shared those fears with me, "I'm terrified by the thought of my child going off to college alone. I felt so confident getting the boys through high school. Everything has changed so much so quickly! Going away to college is foreign to me now.

"When I try to tell Jesse things he should consider when picking a college, he really just nods and then ignores me. I'm afraid that he'll be hurt, confused, and lost without us nearby to guide him. What if he doesn't make friends and connections and feels like he's an outsider?

"I've talked to the Guidance Counselor about my concerns, but he brushes me off and tells me that all kids have to go through this. What if he has to 'play along to get along,' like Noah did at OSU, what if he begins to believe the liberal ideology and forgets the core values he was raised with? I won't be able to really tell if he's ok unless I go to see him. That takes time and is expensive. Also, he thinks it's embarrassing to have his mother visiting him all of the time.

"If he doesn't connect with a church or other Christian kids right away, he's going to drift away from his relationship with God. The influences at college may be too much. Noah told us that most of the boys spend all of their time online playing video games and gambling, or watching porn. They also use drugs and drink a lot. Who is going to help Jesse through this?"

Questionnaire for Parents:

Check the statements or questions that are a "yes" for you, then go on to the next section of scenarios and do the same. Write any thoughts, ideas, or questions that come to your mind in the margin space provided.

- ❑ Have you spent hours talking to friends that have children leaving for college that just don't share your fears and think everything is going to be the way it was when they went to college?
- ❑ When you called the college admissions office, were you told (by what sounded like student workers) that your child would be fine once they get to campus because the University takes care of everything?
- ❑ Did the pastor of your local church assure you that your child has a firm spiritual foundation because they have been so active in youth activities throughout High School?
- ❑ Have you read books on the Freshman Year, but they didn't address the issue of students surviving liberal ideology; only simple things like negotiating cleaning schedules and managing a budget using a credit card?
- ❑ Were you left helpless to advise your child when he told you that the counseling center only has time to facilitate groups, for which none are offered that address this student's (conservative) concerns?
- ❑ If a church near the campus offers social gatherings and activities, is your student unlikely to attend alone, without an established peer group?

- ☐ If your student is shy and introverted, by nature, will they have the ability to start their own conservative peer group in the residence hall on their own?
- ☐ Do you feel blocked every time you reach out to a campus resource by finding that every office requires sensitivity training that includes topics such as "white privilege," "trans pride," and "economic disparity gap (anti-capitalism)"; and that any counter points discussed are considered hostile to the group and require 'trigger warnings'?
- ☐ Are the most disheartening conversations with your child those that end with, "*Mom*, it's not going to be that bad! I can handle it!"
- ☐ Have you been told that the academic department at your child's college has too many incoming students to isolate and reach out to individual students?
- ☐ Are you constantly being told, "Everything will be alright," but in your gut you just don't feel it?
- ☐ Do you feel guilty that you just don't believe that your child is resilient enough to thrive on their own?
- ☐ Do you think that you're the only parent who doesn't believe the promise by the University that "We're here for your student"?
- ☐ In your mind, do you picture your child eating alone, studying alone, and sitting in their tiny dorm room becoming more and more isolated because they can't connect?
- ☐ Is your MaMa Bear self screaming, "They just don't have the maturity yet to cope with everything they're going to be faced with as a conservative on a progressive campus!"?

- ❑ Do you feel confused when and where you should draw the line and make your child make more decisions for themselves?
- ❑ Does doubt gnaw at you wondering that maybe your child *should* learn these new values in order to be successful in the business world?
- ❑ Are you exhausted knowing that instead of sending your child off to college assured they will have a great time growing and learning, that you'll still be parenting 24/7 just like you did when they were in High School?
- ❑ Would you like to connect with other parents on a regular basis, but have no way of contacting them or knowing if they will be supportive?
- ❑ Are you considering paying for a private therapist just to ensure your child has a sympathetic ear and not become depressed or get into bad habits or think about self-harm?
- ❑ Are you afraid your child's values and faith will be challenged on their University campus?
- ❑ Would you like to celebrate your student's successes in their new campus life rather than feeling your heartstrings pulled by their uncertainty and lack of confidence?
- ❑ Is your biggest fear getting a distressed phone call from your child who's away at college? You would give anything to make everything better for them, but you don't know how.
- ❑ Can you imagine sleeping peacefully knowing that someone else has your child's best interest at the center of everything they do?

- ❑ Would you love to join a monthly meeting of like-minded parents who have conservative Christian students going away to college for the first time?
- ❑ Do you know of someone you can turn to when you need experienced advice, but are not sure what questions to ask?
- ❑ You've spent 18 years investing in your child's health, growth, academic success, values and morals, now they're leaving for college. Are you afraid they will be negatively influenced by the progressive, liberal culture at school?
- ❑ Are you worried your child will turn away from God and fall into the typical bad behavior of most college students, losing sight of their established morals and values?
- ❑ Do you dream of having a personal advisor at your fingertips to guide you through your child's first, second, or third year of college?
- ❑ Would you rather celebrate with your student instead of spending another four years nagging and worrying about them?

Angela's scenarios. Check those that resonate with you.

- ❑ Checking her phone again for a text reply from Jesse leaves Angela feeling fearful and anxious. Jesse is an introvert and it takes him a long time to make friends. She knows it's been hard for him to leave the High School peer group that resonates with his values and beliefs. She worries that at college he'll isolate again, walking to class and eating alone. Angela knows that before she was his only lifeline, but it's drained her emotionally and spiritually.

- ❑ Todd, Angela's husband, shares her concerns about Jesse, but is very busy at work and needs to pack for yet another business trip to the west coast. He has little time to offer her the support she desires, and seems annoyed that she's bringing up her fears once again. She's left feeling as isolated as she believes Jesse will be on campus. She hates these misunderstandings with Todd and wishes he could spend more time focusing on their family's needs.
- ❑ Angela is in the kitchen cleaning up after dinner when Jesse Facetimes from college. Jesse is sitting on his dorm room bed, listening to his friends gathering for a floor cooking class down the hall. He's too exhausted today to face another dorm program, a multi-cultural cooking class, that will make him feel bad that he's a privileged white male college student with a bright future.
- ❑ At a church women's Bible study, Angela tries to bring up the subject that she's worried that her children will be influenced by their college campus' liberal ideology. The side-eye looks and jokes about being a conspiracy theorist left her feeling defeated and a little unsure of herself, and what she knew to be true. She leaves the Bible study dragging her confidence behind her. Surely a Bible study is the most appropriate place to seek support and Christian-based answers, isn't it?
- ❑ Todd and Angela's youngest child, Sarah, is a Sophomore in High School. She is furious that Angela will be missing yet another volleyball tournament this weekend because she's driving to Lincoln for *another* campus visit with Jesse. The seven-hour drive isn't that bad, Angela tells herself. It gives her time to make a dent in her Audible book library, and will have time alone talking with Jesse. Yet, her subconscious mind

is unsettled knowing that she's sacrificing supporting and celebrating Sarah's development and achievements, as well as spending otherwise budgeted money on travel expenses and hotel rooms. It's a double-edged sword that doesn't seem to have a win-win solution, but her gut tells her that she must know as much about the people at the University as she can.

WHAT'S YOUR RISE STUDENT COACHING SCORE?

Scoring:

1-10	**You've got this!**
11-20	**You have some anxiety and questions and need more support.**
21-35	**RISE Coaching for Parents is for YOU!**

Angela's comments at the conclusion of the school year, having participated in RISE Coaching for Parents.

- I feel so relaxed knowing that Jesse will have friends and activities already established before he gets to campus for the first time.
- I feel confident knowing that Jesse has a path to success already laid out for him before he leaves for college.
- Todd and I spent last night at our date night dinner talking about *our* goals, knowing that Jesse has a development plan written out and ready when he leaves for school.

- I feel great that Jesse had his first Zoom call with his new RISE student peer group. There are a couple of guys he thinks he can be friends with.
- My golf game is back to where it was and I'm a superstar in my league. I'm not distracted with worry about Jesse leaving for college.
- I feel at peace that I haven't felt the need to travel to Lincoln every couple of months, and have really been there for my daughter at home when she needed my time and attention.
- Breathing through my yoga poses has been so relaxing this year without constant nervous thoughts about how Jesse will do at school. Being present with breath and sweat has never felt so good.
- It's a huge burden off my shoulders knowing that Jesse has connected with a community group and church before he even leaves for college.
- It feels good to go to sleep knowing that I have my own support group to rely on, and Zoom meetings scheduled with these other parents.
- I sit quietly before I go to bed, knowing that my life is so blessed and I've done everything possible to help Jesse through his first year of college.

RISE Student Coaching is an ideal way to support students and parents as they navigate through a liberal college experience. Coaching provides students with an impartial advisor and advocate, and parents a support system so they can celebrate their time being collegiate parents, with less worry.

RESOURCING THROUGH APP & SOCIAL MEDIA

It's the undeniable truth that students are connected through social media and electronics. What can be considered a social challenge for students can also be their connection to a world that accepts them and understands them. What it requires is intention and discernment for them to choose social media that will support their views and values and to disconnect and ignore those that don't. This can be a challenge for students. They have a desire to connect with their peer group whether it be on campus or worldwide because now a worldwide social group is a possibility for them. However, with guidance, planning, and RISE Student Coaching, they can wisely connect with and choose the social media that will benefit, support, and be advantageous to them.

There are apps, such as RISE Student Coaching, that students can download that can connect them to like-minded students across the world. They have activities and action ideas, or solutions to problems at their fingertips anytime. Anytime they're in a difficult situation, they pick up their phone and tap the app and find a resource. If their professor is talking about the foolishness of the conservative view on the federal budget, for example, a student could easily tap their app and search for an appropriate and intelligent response that they can calmly interject into the conversation with the professor or with their peer group. Apps can connect them with other groups and they can interact live with each other. Small groups form around interests or affinities. Students need not feel alone and isolated. They simply need to be guided toward the resources that will support them through their college experience.

It's widely known and understood that a student will not spend time invested in something that they won't receive a payoff. Their time is precious. They feel overwhelmed when they view the number of syllabi they have, the assignments they need to read, the papers they need to write, and the study groups that they need to be involved in. To ask them to be involved in one more group or have one more assignment is understandably tipping the scale. It's imperative to help them to understand the importance of prioritizing the time that they spend in positive groups, in helpful social media outlets, and in supportive Zoom calls.

It can be persuasively presented to students by telling them that, "This is a priority to you and to your mental health, and to your success in college; similar to the time that you invest in studying, the time that you invest in your religious practices such as going to church, and time that you spend developing your social life. It's like brushing your teeth or combing your hair." The time that they devote to their own support will pay off in the end. Designing a support system and a support plan for them so they understand that it is a priority is necessary. This is helping them to understand and prioritize the things that they need to do to be successful. Students are motivated by success! It's what they all want, to walk out with a degree and be prepared for a job. They want to be prepared for the world and these are the tools that will help them prepare. They don't need to feel that they're swimming in a world alone.

It is recommended that students have at least one support app, one support group on Facebook or Instagram, and one Zoom small peer group of students with similar interests, challenges and beliefs.

ACTION LEADS TO EMPOWERMENT

One faculty member said, "I wish these students would fight back. Conservative students won't speak up - they are silenced. They are dropping out of school because they don't believe they have any respect in the classroom or on campus." There is little data that shows that conservatives, and white males specifically, are leaving higher education in droves, because it shows the negative consequences of the campus culture on students. Until half the country accepts this and sends their kids to conservative colleges and then enrollment will plunge, higher education will realize it has to change.

There is hope and that hope is standing up. It's imperative that as adult leaders, parents, clergy faculty, staff, neighbors, and fellow congregants we join together and do their part in deprogramming our young people and supporting those who have found a way to stand up against the woke wave. We need to have determined voices. We need to teach everyone how to speak clearly and confidently.

How do we unite our voices? How do we communicate a call to action? In today's world with social media and computers in the palm of our hands, how do we not unite? How do we not call out for our fellow citizens to join our movement? How do we motivate our young adults to speak confidently when they've watched cities burn, campuses smashed, their peers shouted down, pushed, shoved, spat on and "canceled"? They've seen statues made of marble and stone of our founding fathers toppled and broken into pieces. How do these students, having been isolated, disrespected, and labeled on campus find the courage and the language to stand up and speak up against the woke messages?

There is a movement to have at least one conservative student group on every campus that is organized, active, and willing to stand up for their ideas and beliefs. Students need to activate, communicate, and support each other. There is strength in numbers and a constant presence by conservative students on campus that communicate their conviction that their voice be heard. Encourage voting on campus, local, state, and federal elections. Research candidates' election records and positions on policies. Be the most informed students on campus! Conservatives stand for the opposite of the "herd mentality." They are bright and thoughtful. They make a difference.

Some of the college organizations are:

- College Republicans
- Young America's Foundation
- Turning Point USA
- Young Americans for Liberty
- Leadership Institute
- PragerFORCE
- Your campus ROTC

Encourage your student to be informed and to get involved. The best way to be empowered is to move into action and to activate others.

CHAPTER 7

Where to Begin: Challenge and Support

"If the challenge is too great and the student is not ready for the challenge, a student may go into a state of retreat, where they cease to develop and pull away from the challenge" (Evans, 2010).

Environments that are weighted too heavily in the direction of challenge without adequate support are toxic and they promote defensiveness and anxiety. Those weighted too heavily towards support without adequate challenge are ultimately boring. They promote lifelessness and imbalance that may lead to withdrawal. In contrast, the balance of support and challenge leads to vital engagement.

How do we ensure that our students are offered both the challenges and support that they need to thrive in college? It's understood that students who aspire to earn a college degree have a purpose in mind and are willing to live up to the challenge. However, the challenges that they are experiencing on campuses today are nothing like the academic or social challenges that they faced in high school, or that their parents experienced decades ago. They struggle with fitting into a woke culture, progressive professors, and a woke living environment. These challenges can clearly be far more than these students are prepared for. Like achieving any great goal, it requires strategy, hard work, supportive guidance and coaching with a clear goal.

Here are some suggestions for challenging your student to push them outside of their realm of experience or out of their comfort zone. Oftentimes when we encounter a new situation or environment, we retreat into behavior patterns or experiences that are familiar. The goal here is to gently encourage your students to be challenged and to embrace the challenge in this new environment and this new world that they're living in.

1) *Feel Your Feelings*

   You may have a child that is not at all afraid to feel their feelings boldly and loudly and broadly anywhere anytime. Many students entering college are likely to protect themselves. They may publicly rant over a simple indignation with a roommate or a professor, but their real feelings of fear and isolation may be more difficult for them to identify and express. Challenging them to feel their feelings and to identify exactly what they are and where they're coming from is extremely helpful to support your child and to challenge them.

2) *Think Big*

   Remind them to keep their eyes on the prize and remember the big picture. Oftentimes when students are looking at their syllabi and assignments they become overwhelmed with all the little details such as how many pages was that paper supposed to be and how many pages was I supposed to read in my textbook this week. Encourage them and challenge them to dream big and think big. Remember the big picture. If they have a dream and a goal, anything from composing music, or becoming an astronaut, encourage them to visualize that big picture every day and challenge them to remember why they are enrolled in college and what their dreams are. Help them to remember that excited child in them that is invigorated and thrilled to be going to college. The world is available to them.

3) *Help Others*

The easiest way for a student to regain balance and get out of their own head and stop focusing on their fears and anxieties is to help others. Every campus has a volunteer Resource Center. If they're unable to think of or find something on their own that they're drawn to do, those offices on campus are an excellent resource. They are able to sign up at the Volunteer Resource Center office for as many hours a week or a month as they would like. There's a wide variety of community agencies, churches or shelters that would welcome volunteer hours from students. Also remind them that in helping others they're helping themselves. These opportunities also look great on a resume or job application so it helps them in a number of ways.

4) Encourage them to rely on support other than their parents. It's great when they text and call and check in, of course you want those connections with your children and you want them to know that you're supporting them. This is not the time to cut off that support that they've known to rely on. Now *is* the time for them to learn to stretch and to start asking for help from others.

Finding support elsewhere is building internal resources. We're not asking them to jump into the deep end of the pool; we're asking them to wade in from the shallow end and start taking some steps toward self-reliance. The ability to find resources outside of those that they're comfortable with that they're familiar with is a useful developmental challenge.

Support

Support seems pretty easy for parents. You've been supporting your child for a couple of decades! You can help your student now make the transition into college by expanding their support system. It's putting more responsibility into their lap while giving them the communication and understanding that you are always there for them.

1) *Make a Plan*

So often, parents are under the belief that once they drop their student off at college that everything will flow for them. When, in fact, students have so much to do for themselves to prepare for this overwhelming job of moving away they often underestimate its impact. Help them to make a plan. Have a planner and get organized.

Students will oftentimes have their first meeting with their academic department or advisor. That's a very critical time for them that first week on campus. 'Start making connections' needs to be in the plan. Define for the student that this is a priority and it must be done the first two weeks on campus. Some academic departments will not make appointments with students the first week because campus is just opening for the year and they're very overwhelmed. It's okay. Have students find any person that can see them. It may be the department administrative assistant. Then make that connection with the administrative assistant! Ask to look around the building and the classrooms. Ask questions. Doing this will connect the students so they feel like they belong. A schedule for sleeping should be in the plan, as well as a schedule for socializing, a schedule for religious practices, including worship and volunteer opportunities. The more defined their plan before the student goes to campus, the more successful they're going to be.

Students will more than likely vary from the plan. They're going to waver and that's to be expected. The reality of campus and the demands on their time are all going to be things that they're not going to anticipate. But with a plan, once things feel like they're going off the rails you can direct them back to their plan. When they start feeling overwhelmed and saying, 'you know, oh my gosh, I don't have time for all these things,' ask them to go back and look at their plan. Talk about which parts of the plan (and the planner they are using) are working and which aren't. Adapt it. These are all fabulous support conversations that parents can have with students.

2) *Ask for Help*

This seems like a no-brainer, but it's shocking how hard this is for students. It's going outside of their comfort zone, so they will need to be reminded to ask for help. They can ask you for help and you can tell them that it's okay that they ask you for help. Then you may direct them to other resources. They need to reach out and tell someone when they're stuck. Every day that they sit stuck is a day that's passing by that they're getting behind. It's a day that passes by and their anxiety is increasing. It's a day that goes by that they're starting to feel defeated. We want to avoid losing any days with our students on campus.

They need to know that every day that they're asking for help is a success, and it's moving them forward.

3) *Get Involved*

One of the best things you can do to support your student is to encourage them to get involved on campus. Campus may be overwhelming with woke activities and student groups, but it's not impossible for your student to get involved. There are interest groups, academic groups, and social groups. Getting involved connects a student to their campus, to a peer group, and helps them connect with themselves and their evolving identity. Getting involved for many students is going to be the memories that they take with them after they leave the campus. They may not remember the courses they took, but they will remember the activities that they were involved in.

4) *Support Your Student*

Encourage your student to *keep a gratitude list or journal daily*. As has been proven through studies and anecdotal conversations, we all know that when we're grateful we're happier, we're more productive, we're more balanced, and we're more grounded. Students can have very dark days, they can have very bad days; days that they just feel everything is lost. Encouraging them to keep a gratitude list or journal is a simple way to help them offset the times that things become overwhelming for them. Before they leave for campus, give them a gratitude journal or an app on their phone. It may be as simple as just keeping a list of the 'Sunny Side' things that happen each day. These lists can be as simple as 'they served the best tacos in the dining hall today,' or, 'a guy or girl that I've been admiring smiled at me as we passed on the sidewalk.' Those little things can be a lifeline for students when they're feeling overwhelmed and anxious.

5) *Find a Coach*

Students and parents don't need to do this alone. One of the most supportive things you can do for you and your student is to hire a coach that's there for them every day. A RISE coach provides guidelines for them so they can see where they're going and be able to look back and see where they've been. It's someone who can be a resource for things such as communication. They can offer students directions on how to talk to other students about complicated and difficult issues. Coaching can make all the difference for a student. So often they're reluctant to reach out to peers (or their parents) for support, and let's face it, peer support is limited and unreliable. If they're reluctant to go to an academic advisor or professor, they may need encouragement and coaching prior to approaching the instructor to 'play out' some scenarios or communication alternatives. The same is true with housing issues. Any challenge that they have on campus and with the campus community will always be supported by a coach. Students need a coach who is independent of their family, their church community, their college community, and is someone they can trust who will listen to them, is non-judgmental, and someone they can rely on and go to for guidance and clear action steps. With RISE Student Coaching, they will also receive the benefit of a Zoom community of peers, and the RISE Coaching App. These resources offer students across the country the ability to offer each other support and guidance whenever needed.

STRONG PARENTS

Sorry to say this mom and dad, but you have been sold a bill of goods. You've been told that in order for your children to be happy and successful the parents must follow along with the "progressive 'in' crowd" in order to be good parents. Nothing could be further from the truth. Parents know more by following their own gut instinct than any trend will ever prove true or helpful.

In the 1950s, it was trendy to feed an infant only formula because formula was the new scientifically improved way to feed a baby that far exceeded nursing mother's milk which had ensured the survival of the species for millions of years. As always, the pendulum swings, and by the 1980s nursing babies was the foundation of a nurturing and healthy parent-child relationship. Now, mothers who had to or chose to feed with a bottle and formula were dismissed as bad mothers. By the 2000s, nursing stations had been installed in most major social gathering places, and a movement was launched for nursing children openly in public spaces.

Trends come and go. What one needs to highly consider is one's own common sense. Is the newest trend really the best trend because it's a popular belief? Is it the best belief? Could it be possible that the faster a trend sweeps through, the less reliable it could be? Of course we all know the answer to that is yes, that's true. Tried and true *is* more reliable along with the great benefit of evolving thought and ideas. It's a balance that parents are capable of and challenged to master.

Students will benefit from a foundation that comes from strong, assured, confident parents. That's a tall bill to fill in today's culture. With the remote control one can flip through thousands of channels, and with every turn of the channel one will be shown extreme socially acceptable behaviors, morals and beliefs. Parents are implicitly being told that all of those images and messages are okay for their child to explore and for parents to accept. The internet provides an infinite amount of opportunity to discover any number of images, videos, and information on parenting.

The question that parents need to sleep on at night is what choices do they feel confident that their child can make for themselves. Would they feel confident about their 15-year-old going to war? Probably not. Parents have been placed in children's lives explicitly in order to guide their children to lead them to lead productive lives and to be contributors to society.

When parents drop their students off on their university campus, the very first day everyone's hopes are high. They smile and wave goodbye, they hug and cry. They don't have any idea what's going to happen once the door closes behind the child going into their dorm. Children don't know, and don't know the questions to ask until it's being experienced and by then it's too late. When students are living on their own for the first time, most of them flounder, at least just a bit.

Strong parents know what's going to happen before their children arrive at college. So many parents assume it's the same kind of campus environment that they left decades ago. That is no longer true. Evolution has happened at a breakneck speed. Even over the last decade, the campus culture is nearly unrecognizable.

Strong parents know what to do when things start 'going south' for their children. Strong parents are not standing alone, but have a supportive and collaborative support system of parents upon whom they can rely. That collaborative support system has to be nurtured and developed prior to students arriving on campus. Trust must be developed. Parents must be restored to their natural rights and position as authority figures, wise protectors, champions and cheerleaders, and at times gladiators that will fight off the system in order to protect their children.

Strong parents are the foundation of student success on campus. Too often parents don't know until it's too late that they are lacking in wisdom, language, and understanding of what's going on behind the scenes for their student. Preparation prior to students heading to campus is the key to strong parents and central to their students' success. Parenting tips and guidelines can be found from a number of resources such as reading books or videos and podcasts. More helpful to gain a deep understanding of campus life is talking with parents who have students already on campus and asking what their experience has been. Joining a collaborative group, such as the RISE Student Coaching program that provides guidance and ensures that all participants gain the most benefit from the coaching program.

Parents need advocates. Parents commonly turn to their spouse or co-parent. When disagreements in approaches or behavioral interventions arise, it creates a rift within the parents' relationship. This is not beneficial to the student; this does not create a strong parental center upon which the student can rely. This is a benefit of a facilitated coaching program that one or both parents can participate in and receive guidance and support that is ongoing and consistent.

Parents are expected to know it all. To do it all. To be experts in everything, when they have no experience or skills to do so. It is a wise investment for parents to reach out to prepare for the challenges they will surely encounter as their students enter college.

Strong parents are informed. Strong parents are confident. Strong parents have developed all the skills necessary to be resilient themselves. Strong parents can model communication skills and self-advocacy abilities for their child. The days have passed when parents can innocently drop their children off at campus and trust that their child will receive the best experience possible. Instead, it's necessary that parents prepare and accept a growth trajectory for *themselves* throughout their child's college career.

Despite the stress of having a college student in their lives, parents can remain strong and offer support. Even with all of the changes and potential challenges that come with monitoring learning, or navigating dorm life, parents should strive to maintain open lines of communication and extend virtual hugs now more than ever. It's important for both parent and student to understand that there is no "right" way to handle this new reality; rather, it's about developing healthy habits together, such as setting goals for each day or week, adjusting achievable expectations depending on how the student is feeling, and checking in frequently.

Parents also need to be mindful of their own well-being during this time – making sure to take breaks from worrying about their child by engaging in self-care activities. Doing so sets a positive example for college students and encourages them to take the same measures for their own mental health. Overall, no matter how difficult it can be at times, parents of college students remain strong and resilient in order to provide the best support they can during these unprecedented times.

With love, patience and understanding, parents will help their college students navigate this season with grace. No matter if they're living away from home or learning remotely, now is the perfect time to remind them how much you care about them and that they are not alone throughout this journey. Showing your support will go a long way towards helping your children feel safe and secure during this tumultuous period in their lives – proving that, no matter how difficult things can get, parents of college students remain strong and steadfast in their care for their children.

Self-care and personal mental health will ground parents. Here are a few suggestions to assist in that challenge.

1. *Control*

Concern vs. Influence – You CHOOSE!

Know the difference between what you can and can't change. You might be "concerned" that there is a possibility that a hurricane could develop near your city. You have no influence over the weather, and cannot change the course of the storm. You choose to either wait and worry filled with anxiety and distress, or resolve to do what can be done to prepare, and allow the rest to be determined by God. You recognize the limits of your control and have a realistic understanding of choosing to give your best effort no matter what. You are patient and make realistic plans within your circle of control.

Students will encounter situations that will feel to them as imposing as a hurricane bearing down off a nearby shore. Viewing change or challenge as an opportunity for growth guides them and encourages them to have confidence in themselves and focus on the things they can control and have positive influence over.

2. *Commitment*

Resolve to hold on to your values and those things that you hold closely. Remain clear and focus on the things that you stand for in life and that are important.

You can make a commitment to keep your values in view and to always support your student.

Your son and his lab partners were so excited sharing their spring break travel plans, they failed to create a care (feeding & watering) schedule for their experimental psych lab rat while they were all gone over break. They wrapped up their last report and submitted it, and let out a group hoot while they rushed out of the lab more than ready to take off to sunny paradise. Over break, it died.

The neglectful suffering of any lab animal is a serious academic offense. When they returned, one of the guys went to the lab to record the weekly outcomes. Finding the rat dead, he texted the other three and told them to drop everything and get there right away. Panicked and ashamed, together they came up with a list of viable lies to cover their mistake. They also came up with a list of likely consequences, and none of them ended well for the lab team. Knowing that they would be given university sanctions that very well could include academic suspension, they agreed on the best excuse, and made an appointment to meet with their professor later that afternoon.

Your son, however, felt sick all day. His moral compass was thrown off by the group of classmates when he agreed to the lie. It just wasn't right. They had been selfishly careless and an animal died because of their foolish distractions. His guilt was overwhelming.

When the group met before their appointment, he told them that he had to admit the truth. He was willing to suffer the consequences, however harsh, because it was the right thing to do and he knew that he would have the support of his parents and friends, even if he was suspended. He would agree to any sanctions and complete his obligations by the deadline so he could move forward with a clean record fall semester. His resilience and resolve was inspiring to the other students. One by one, they agreed to stand together and tell the entire truth and accept the consequences.

Their professor reacted with shock and dismay to the grim account of their negligence. Their case was referred to the Dean for formal action. Two weeks dragged by as each student tried not to freak out while they withstood the anger and disappointment of their parents, and stressed about their future at the university.

The Dean listened. She frowned. She shook her head in disgust. The young men held their breath as she closed her laptop and sat back in her chair. After a long pause, she sighed deeply, and began to explain to them her determination. Because they showed great maturity in facing their egregious mistake, she was willing to recommend the lightest sanction possible. They were assigned an incomplete for the semester, rather than a fail or academic suspension, and were required to retake the course the following semester as well as serve as lab assistants caring for the animals throughout all weekends and breaks.

The young men were near tears. Their gratitude overflowed. They shared their story with all of their friends as a testament to truth and justice. They were able to walk through campus with self-confidence, knowing that they were capable of facing hardship and overcoming it by standing firm in doing what was right.

There are times when your child will be faced with the most challenging circumstances or situations. These are times that the struggle becomes epic and they will have to exercise personal and spiritual strength.

These are the times that they will rely on their commitment to their foundation of morals and values and their commitment to do what's right and honorable. They will rely on the consistency and commitment of their parents. These difficult times and situations are the time that commitment matters the most.

3. *Challenge*

Expect barriers and setbacks and learn to see them as an opportunity for learning.

Your daughter is an accomplished flutist and her focus has been like laser vision on sitting in the first chair in the chamber ensemble. She signed up for special instruction, rehearsed every spare minute she had, and even gave practice performances for students in her residence hall. She was nervous, but ready for her audition.

One thing was niggling in her mind, though. A new student had transferred in this semester, and seemed to be really good, although they had never played together before. The chamber ensemble was small, and only a few musicians were selected for this elite concert group. They would have the opportunity to travel to other campuses to perform and one amazing trip to Spain was planned as an academic exchange.

Preparation was everything. Rehearse, rehearse, rehearse! She felt her lips were stuck in a permanent flutist embouchure.

The night before the audition, she walked into her dorm room to find her roommate sprawled across the floor, seemingly unconscious. She shook her and yelled her name into her pale ashen face. She opened the door into the hallway and screamed for help. The RA ran in and reached above the desk to retrieve an epipen from the shelf. Another student was dialing 911 on her cell phone. As the antidote was slowly relieving her symptoms, her ability to speak came back. Yes, she'd go to the hospital to get checked out, but no, she knew she'd be fine. Yes, they should get her cell phone and call her mother, but no, her mother shouldn't drive three hours just to see her released from the hospital and brought back to her dorm room.

After the frenzy died down, the audition once again took center stage. Rest and sleep was all she could do now. Easier said than done. Wide awake, she heard her roommate return at 1:45 AM. The rest of the night was a twist of covers and whirling fears.

The audition didn't go badly; it was dreadful. Now stressed, exhausted, and nerves worn by multiple surges of adrenaline over the past 12 hours, her fingers didn't respond to her mind's commands. Her performance was flat and lifeless.

The news was offered to her with great sensitivity; not only had she *not* earned 1st chair, she was not selected for the ensemble at all. Feeling as though she was having a migraine, her senses exploded, and shut down all at once. Dreaming of this achievement had been all she had worked for for the past two years. Silent tears streamed down her cheeks as she blindly reached down and collected her things. Robotically walking down the sidewalk, she sat down on a bench and dialed her mother. When no sound could be heard, you, as her mother, knew. The harrowing experience during the night combined with the heightened competition level raised by the more accomplished flutist worked to create an audition challenge which she had not experienced before and her abilities could not rise to conquer.

Together, over the next few weeks, you worked out a plan to audition for a different group, the chamber orchestra. It was bigger and more chairs were available. She was surely prepared and would audition well. Although it was not the dream opportunity she'd hoped and prayed for, it was still an opportunity to grow as a musician and improve her skills.

She sincerely congratulated the flutists that were selected for the chamber ensemble, and wished them well. Although there were moments that envy raised its ugly head, she chose to focus on her strong ability and gratitude for her gifts. She was confident that it had all worked out for the best.

Sometimes circumstances beyond our control influence the outcomes of things our students have worked so hard to achieve. The disappointment is deep. Helping your student to remain focused on their goals, regardless of external influences or situations, gives them the confidence to move forward.

Creating an action plan and reflecting on the situation with a sense of humor can open the door to deeper self confidence and skills to cope with stress and disappointment. Every time your child is able to tolerate and effectively manage their feelings of frustration and impulses toward negativity, they grow stronger and are able to master resilience and resolve in new and more challenging situations.

4. *Connection*

Develop a strong social network - having caring, supportive people around you acts as a protective factor during times of crisis.

Sitting on the floor of his dorm room studying for his biology midterm, your son hears the fire alarm sounding in the hallway. He jumps up and while slipping on his crocks, he grabs his coat, phone, and keys and flies out the door. In the hallway, he hears an unusual sound, but keeps moving toward the exit with the rest of the residents. Once outside, he hears students talking about water in the hallway on the floor above him.

Students shivering in the freezing night air are finally told that a water pipe has burst and several of the rooms are uninhabitable. They will be announced in a few minutes along with information on accommodations for the night.

The list was read. Residents of unaffected rooms filed back into the building. The students whose rooms were called lined up in the foyer of the building to give their name and contact information to the hall staff holding clipboards. Your son was in that line. He was allowed to go up to his room to collect what he needed for an overnight stay before boarding a bus to a local hotel.

Sloshing down the hallway through ankle deep water he approached his room. Opening the door, his heart sank. His study "cubby" on the floor between the bed and the window was under a foot of standing water. Textbooks, notebooks, his laptop, ipad, and his piles of clothes were under water. His head was spinning as he tried to think of what he should take for the night. His backpack was soaked. The things that he used most often were casually dropped on the floor as soon as he entered the room. His clothes fell where he took them off, books were scattered along the wall of his study "cubby."

The phone calls home had gone directly to voicemail. He sat on the edge of his bed and pulled out his phone. At least he had grabbed it on his way out before the flood had reached his floor. He dialed his friend, Sam, who lived in a dorm across campus. Sam was in his fellowship group and was a good friend. He'd know what to do.

Within minutes they had a plan to gather a toothbrush, underwear, socks, and a phone charger. Sam was coming to get him to spend the night at his dorm. His phone chimed as soon as he hung up with Sam. The text was Gabrielle from their fellowship group letting him know the group was meeting tonight and bringing stuff to donate to the students that had been displaced. She wanted him to spread the word to all the residents that might need help.

He left his room and went to tell the RA and the other students that he saw in the hallways. It felt great to have people to rely on when crazy things happened.

Resilient students can engage the support of others because they have already established strong connections within their community.

They are confident and secure in their relationships and know they can count on them for help.

Online relationships are valuable and offer encouragement and support in many important ways. Personal, face-to-face connections are invaluable in times of crisis when it's necessary to rely on others for tangible help and support.

Strategies for Building Resilience You Can Build With Your Child

- Make Connections - caring, supportive relationships: family, friends, groups.
- Avoid seeing crises as insurmountable problems - you can change how you interpret and respond to stressful events.
- Accept that change is part of living - the only thing that is constant in life is change. Reflect on change.
- Move towards your goals, take charge - do something regularly, no matter how small, that enables you to move towards your goals.
- Take decisive action - rather than detaching completely and wishing that problems and stressors would go away.
- Look for opportunities for self-discovery - reflection - people often grow in some respect as a result of their struggle with stressful events.
- Nurture a positive view of yourself - trust your instincts - develop confidence in your ability.
- Pay attention to self identity.
- Keep things in perspective - keep a long-term perspective - avoid blowing things out of proportion.

- Maintain a hopeful outlook, find your sense of purpose - visualize what you want (goals) rather than worry about or focus on what you fear or what you do not have.
- Take care of yourself - pay attention/be mindful of your own needs and feelings.
- Engage in activities you enjoy and find relaxing.

COLLABORATION

Collaborative learning in college is the educational approach of using groups to enhance learning through working together. Groups of two or more learners work together to solve problems, complete tasks, or learn new concepts.

Whether in a work environment, home environment, or social environment, when collaboration is applied a powerful shift takes place. The sum total becomes larger than the amount of the parts. Collaborating participants are able to see things through others' eyes and problem solve in ways that they couldn't alone. They see examples and experiences that they have not had themselves. Through discussions, they deepen their understanding of problems and tribulations.

A great example of this is participating in a book club. Book clubs are very popular and allow people to read a book as an individual alone, in isolation. But the book comes alive when they enter a room and share their insights with others. Although everyone has read the same material they come with different understanding, thoughts and ideas based upon their own experiences. They contribute their own gifts and intelligences. Collaborative learning is one of the highest possible levels of learning.

Collaborative learning happens at all stages of development. In infancy children observe each other and imitate one another. In academia, high level problem solving happens in groups.

Collaborative learning can also be utilized through technology. Using webinars, Zoom meetings, social media, and even apps, the ability to host meetings and groups allows collaborative learning and facilitates deeper growth and understanding. Collaboration can happen over continents, countries, through time zones, and can navigate cultural and language barriers.

Activities and exercises can be executed and accomplished in collaborative teams and reviewed using technology and presentations and small group work. Collaborative learning can be highly structured or very loosely community-based. A strong coaching facilitator will allow participants to explore and grow at their own pace for both students and parents. Collaborative opportunities of learning are ideal in coaching programs for college students.

A student who finds themselves alone and afraid on a college campus will likely not reach out for support. Their trust in the system was shattered early in their university experience. An online resource offers them security and anonymity availability 24 hours a day for them to reach out for help.

Small groups that are offered online will develop into a trusting and supportive student team that offers group problem solving and support. With the structure provided by the RISE Student Coaching program, students can help one another move through developmental stages and through the C's of resilience. They're able to use common language and build a culture of support and understanding.

Parents benefit from a supportive and collaborative community as well. A supportive group of like-minded parents learning together is both highly effective and satisfying. In the company of others with similar concerns and experiences, problem solving and concerns become easier to navigate.

ENGAGED STUDENTS

[52]According to Tony Robbins, "if you're pushing hard against something, it pushes back. You get upset and then try to push harder, but nothing's moving. The more you focus on the problem, the more power you give it. When you put your energy toward creating a fulfilled, happy life, you take power away from the problem and put it toward a solution. You just may find some of your problems fixed themselves.

"Instead of focusing your energy on the problem that's causing you stress and unhappiness, you could be using it to power aspects of your life you actually enjoy. Instead of energizing your problems, you could be channeling that energy to learning how to achieve goals more effectively. Sometimes the best way to solve something is to just let it go. If you let it go, you'll also let go of your suffering."

That's very wise advice and it applies to our conservative students in colleges and universities. Students need to balance their lives and to focus on things that are going well, their successes and their outside interests. It is a balancing act.

[53]College student engagement has numerous benefits, not only for the students themselves, but also for their universities and society as a whole. Research has shown that engaging in activities such as attending lectures, participating in clubs or societies, and volunteering can lead to improved academic performance, better career prospects and increased satisfaction with college life. Additionally, student engagement can create a sense of community amongst students and promote positive relationships amongst peers. It can provide an outlet for creative expression and help foster personal development. By taking part in such activities, students are able to acquire valuable skills which they

52 www.RISEstudentcoaching.com/resources

53 www.RISEstudentcoaching.com/resources

may go on to use in their professional lives after graduation. Ultimately, fostering student engagement is beneficial not only to individual students but also to a wider society as a whole. It is therefore critical that parents encourage and support student engagement.

In order to foster meaningful student engagement, universities need to provide a range of resources and opportunities for students to get involved. This can include providing access to mentors or alumni who can offer guidance and advice, as well as offering internships or research projects that allow students to gain practical experience. Universities should strive to create an environment which allows individuals with diverse backgrounds and abilities to participate and thrive, including conservative ideas and values. Through such measures, universities can ensure that all students are able to benefit from engaging in university life, thus enabling them to achieve their full potential both while they are at college and afterwards.

ONLINE COMMUNITIES

Online communities can provide college students with a wide range of benefits. With the help of these communities, students are able to meet and connect with peers who have similar interests or experiences. This leads to meaningful friendships being formed and allows for a sense of belonging that may not otherwise be felt on campus. Having access to an online community gives college students the opportunity to share advice and discuss their challenges, successes and experiences in a safe setting. These insights can prove invaluable when it comes to making informed decisions about their social and academic pursuits. Additionally, many online communities may focus on career development and offer resources such as internships, job postings and networking opportunities which can help put them on track towards achieving their goals after graduation. Ultimately, college students stand to benefit greatly from joining and engaging in an online community that is supportive and rich with resources.

The RISE Student community offers students a variety of opportunities to engage online. Their RISE Cohort, or small group, meet regularly and they also have the ability to connect with others anytime they need support. Through Zoom call groups and the RISE Student Coaching app, connections and collaboration is at their fingertips.

RETREATS

Summer retreats are offered through the RISE Student Coaching program. Students gather in small groups at the retreat to gain support, learn skills, become familiarized and prepared for the experience that they will encounter once they arrive on campus. These small group cohorts will become their Zoom group which will meet ongoing throughout the year. These relationships will become critical and central to their college experience. Although students will be going to a variety of campuses to be enrolled in a variety of majors, they will have a strong relationship and partnership with their RISE Cohort. This cohort will remain in place throughout their entire college experience. If they choose, they could remain connected throughout graduate school and into their lives, as often does happen.

The summer retreats will be well supervised by RISE Coaches. Students can build a relationship with their coaches throughout the retreat. Activities that are engaging, interesting, and are developing their skills will be highlighted each day. Much like the summer camp that they've been familiar with as a youth, this is an age-appropriate retreat that is designed and developed for the students entering college.

Retreats will also be offered consecutive summers as cohort groups advance through their college career. Building on the skills that they have developed in previous years, they will prepare for the next steps in their college career. Significant and distinct decisions and experiences happen over a student's freshman year, their sophomore year, their junior year, and their senior year.

Freshman year focuses on fitting in on campus, understanding the academic rigors and how to master time management and study skills, and developing an individual identity away from their parents' home.

Sophomore year, students are looking for leadership opportunities that provide growth and the ability to contribute to their communities. Tutoring and mentorship opportunities are important during a student's sophomore year.

Junior year students are searching for internships, focusing on improving their grade point average, and finding ways to begin making adult decisions, such as living independently.

Senior year students are focusing on their resume to secure employment, or applying to graduate schools, and taking graduate entrance exams.

Attending the RISE Student Coaching summer retreats with their cohort group each summer supports students as they progress through their development and academic status.

RISE COACH TRAINING PROGRAM - PASS IT ON AND GROW

The benefits of a RISE Coach training program are diverse and far-reaching. This type of program equips trainers, teachers, and coaches with the necessary skills to effectively lead and manage learning experiences for their coaching students. This enables coaches to foster an environment of collaboration and knowledge sharing—promoting coaching success by addressing key areas, such as:

- Mastering the RISE Student Coaching program curriculum
- Enhancing communication between coaches and students
- Increasing coaching confidence in their presentation skills
- Providing constructive feedback for continued improvement
- Improving understanding on how to tailor coaching modules to individual student needs
- Developing new approaches to delivering successful training outcomes

These gains can be seen both in terms of the immediate outcomes from individual coaching skills as well as the long-term benefit of having a well-developed curriculum to draw from. Well-trained coaches who are supported and nurtured by a RISE Coach training program will help ensure that skills are taught effectively, while also supporting coaches in their business endeavors. By investing in this type of training, coaches are investing in the success of their business as well as the students they lead.

In addition, coaches that invest in the RISE Coach training program can develop strong relationships with other coaches, leading to improved understanding and collaboration. Through Zoom RISE Coaches groups, coaches develop knowledge and effective strategies, which means there is more capacity for successful implementations of new ideas, processes or products—ultimately leading to increased productivity and better results working with students and parents.

Helping others is a calling. Working in higher education is also a calling. Anyone who has worked with college students knows the excitement, the passion and the fulfillment that comes with working with these students every single day. You see the future standing before you and that's a thrill and an honor. It's one that I enjoyed for nearly two decades. It's the reason that I have created this book. Not only did I want to help students and parents navigate the challenging experiences they face on college campuses today, but also to inspire professionals who are seeking an alternative to the public school system (K-12), traditional higher education, and others that are in the coaching field already.

I've created a training program for coaches to work with parents and students in colleges and universities. This is my ultimate passion; to utilize my experience, knowledge and skills in higher education, student development, and coaching and training. This training program is exciting and prepares any coach to work with parents and students offering a step-by-step guide, curriculum, materials, developed technology, and ongoing support and coaching.

The RISE Coach training program will inspire and leave any coach with confidence and preparedness. If you love what you've seen in this book and your heart is moved to make the world a better place and help students move through this process - this career will be for you.

Do you see yourself each day waking up knowing that you will have a significant impact on the lives of our future leaders? Would you love to wake up and start each day knowing that you can ease the burden, the stress and anxiety of our college students? Would you love to wake up each day and know that a parent has slept more peacefully that night knowing that their child's pathway to success has been established and is being monitored by a coaching professional with a strong background in student development coaching and training? Wouldn't it be fantastic to know that our future leaders, our future clergy, our future political leaders, our future teachers, our future mothers and fathers, have had the support and guidance of enthusiastic, passionate RISE Coach throughout these very challenging college years? Helping others to grow is a reward in itself. Choosing a career as a RISE Coach can be your pathway to success and fulfillment.

READER BONUS!

Dear Reader,

Learn the basics of resilience and engagement skills for college students so you can prepare yourself and your child for a fruitful academic year. Download a free copy of "College Survival Guide for Conservatives: 5 Easy and Practical Tips for Parents" along with a bonus coaching video at www.risestudentcoaching.com.

Discover the essential foundations of resilience and engagement skills specifically designed for college students, equipping both you and your child with the necessary tools for a successful and fulfilling academic year.

As an added bonus, gain invaluable insights through a coaching video accompanying the guide, ensuring you are well-equipped to navigate the unique challenges and opportunities that lie ahead. Don't miss out on this opportunity to empower yourself and support your child's journey through college.

If we are still giving away this course by the time you're reading this book, head straight over to your computer and start the course now. It's absolutely free and you'll be glad you did.

READER BONUS!

Download the course here: www.risestudentcoaching.com

Made in the USA
Columbia, SC
21 July 2023